FROM COLONIES TO COUNTRY 1735-1791

STUDENT STUDY GUIDE

OXFORD

UNIVERSITY PRESS

OXFORD
UNIVERSITY PRESS

Oxford University Press, Inc., publishes works that
further Oxford University's objective of excellence
in research, scholarship, and education.

Oxford   New York
Auckland   Cape Town   Dar es Salaam   Hong Kong   Karachi
Kuala Lumpur   Madrid   Melbourne   Mexico City   Nairobi
New Delhi   Shanghai   Taipei   Toronto

With offices in
Argentina   Austria   Brazil   Chile   Czech Republic   France   Greece
Guatemala   Hungary   Italy   Japan   Poland   Portugal   Singapore
South Korea   Switzerland   Thailand   Turkey   Ukr°aine   Vietnam

Published by Oxford University Press, Inc.
198 Madison Avenue, New York, NY 10016

Oxford is a registered trademark of Oxford University Press

ISBN 978-0-19-518882-0

Writer: Scott Ingram
Project Manager: Matt Fisher
Project Director: Jacqueline A. Ball
Education Consultant: Diane L. Brooks, Ed.D.
Design: designlabnyc

Casper Grathwohl, Publisher

Printed in the United States of America
on acid-free paper

Dear Parents, Guardians, and Students:

This study guide has been created to increase student enjoyment and understanding of *A History of US*.

The study guide offers a wide variety of interactive exercises to support every chapter. At the back of the guide are activity maps to help tie your study of history to the study of geography. Also, you will find several copies of a library/media center research log to use to organize your time researching projects and assignments. Parents or other family members can participate in activities marked "With a Parent or Partner." Adults can help in other ways, too. One important way is to encourage students to create and use a history journal as they work through the exercises in the guide. The journal can simply be an off-the-shelf notebook or three-ring binder used only for this purpose. Some students might like to customize their journals with markers, colored paper, drawings, or computer graphics. No matter what it looks like, a journal is a student's very own place to organize thoughts, practice writing, and make notes on important information. It will serve as a personal report of ongoing progress that your child's teacher can evaluate regularly. When completed, it will be a source of satisfaction and accomplishment for your child.

Sincerely,

Casper Grathwohl
Publisher

This book belongs to:

_____

CONTENTS

HOW TO USE THE
STUDENT STUDY GUIDES TO
A HISTORY OF US

One word describes A History of US: stories. Every book in this series is packed with stories about people who built a brand new country like none before. You will meet presidents and politicians, artists and inventors, ordinary people who did amazing things and had wonderful adventures. The best part is that all the stories are true. All the people are real.

As you read this book, you can enjoy the stories while you build valuable thinking and writing skills. The book will help you pass important tests. The sample pages below show special features in all the History of US books. Take a look!

Before you read

- Have a notebook or extra paper and a pen handy to make a history journal. A dictionary and thesaurus will help you too.

- Read the chapter title and predict what you will learn from the chapter. Note that often the author often adds humor to her titles with plays on words or **puns**, as in this title.

- Study all maps, photos, and their captions closely. The captions often contain important information you won't find in the text.

27 Howe Billy Wished France Wouldn't Join In

General Howe had already served in America. In 1759 he led Wolfe's troops to seize Quebec.

A ***hoop-stay*** was part of the stiffening in a skirt; a ***jupon*** was part of a corset. ***Matrons*** are married women. The ***misses*** are single girls; ***swains*** and ***beaux*** are young men or boyfriends. ***Making love*** meant flirting. ***British Grenadiers*** are part of the royal household's infantry.

Sir William Howe (who was sometimes called Billy Howe) was in charge of all the British forces in America. It was Howe who drove the American army from Long Island to Manhattan. Then he chased it across another river to New Jersey. And, after that, he forced George Washington to flee on—to Pennsylvania. It looked as if it was all over for the rebels. In New Jersey, some 3,000 Americans took an oath of allegiance to the king. But Washington got lucky again. The Europeans didn't like to fight in cold weather.

Sir William settled in New York City for the winter season. Howe thought Washington and his army were done for and could be

Swarming with Beaux

Rebecca Franks was the daughter of a wealthy Philadelphia merchant. Her father was the king's agent in Pennsylvania, and the family were Loyalists. Rebecca visited New York when it was occupied by the British. Her main interest in the war was that it meant New York was full of handsome officers:

My Dear Abby, By the by, few New York ladies know how to entertain company in their own houses unless they introduce the card tables....I don't know a woman or girl that can chat above half an hour, and that on the form of a cap, the colour of a ribbon or the set of a hoop-stay or jupon....Here, you enter a room with a formal set curtsey and after the how do's, 'tis a fine, or a bad day, and those trifling nothings are finish'd, all's a dead calm till the cards are introduced, when you see pleasure dancing in the eyes of all the matrons....The misses, if they have a favorite swain, frequently decline playing for the pleasure of making love....Yesterday the Grenadiers had a race at the Flatlands, and in the afternoon this house swarm'd with beaux and some very smart ones. How the girls wou'd have envy'd me cou'd they have peep'd and seen how I was surrounded.

126

As you read

- Keep a list of questions.

- Note the bold-faced definitions in the margins. They tell you the meanings of important words and terms – ones you may not know.

- Look up other unfamiliar words in a dictionary.

- Note other sidebars or special features. They contain additional information for your enjoyment and to build your understanding. Often sidebars and features contain quotations from primary source documents such as a diary or letter, like this one. Sometimes the primary source item is a cartoon or picture.

After you read

- Compare what you have learned with what you thought you would learn before you began the chapter.

The next two pages have models of graphic organizers. You will need these to do the activities for each chapter on the pages after that. Go back to the book as often as you need to.

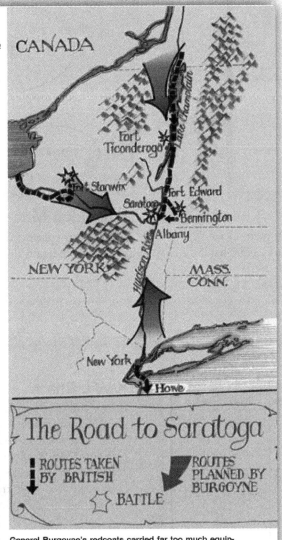

finished off in springtime. Besides, Billy Howe loved partying. And some people say he liked the Americans and didn't approve of George III's politics. For reasons that no one is quite sure of, General Howe just took it easy.

But George Washington was no quitter. On Christmas Eve of 1776, in bitter cold, Washington got the Massachusetts fishermen to ferry his men across the Delaware River from Pennsylvania back to New Jersey. The river was clogged with huge chunks of ice. You had to be crazy, or coolly courageous, to go out into that dangerous water. The Hessians, on the other side—at Trenton, New Jersey— were so sure Washington wouldn't cross in such bad weather that they didn't patrol the river. Washington took them by complete surprise.

A week later, Washington left a few men to tend his campfires and fool the enemy. He quietly marched his army to Prince-ton, New Jersey, where he surprised and beat a British force. People in New Jersey forgot the oaths they had sworn to the king. They were Patriots again.

Those weren't big victories that Washington had won, but they certainly helped American morale. And American morale needed help. It still didn't seem as if the colonies had a chance. After all, Great Britain had the most feared army in the world. It was amazing that a group of small colonies would even attempt to fight the powerful British empire. When a large English army (9,500 men and 138 cannons) headed south from Canada in June 1777, many observers thought the rebellion would soon be over.

The army was led by one of Britain's

The Road to Saratoga

General Burgoyne's redcoats carried far too much equipment. Each man's boots alone weighed 12 pounds. They took two months to cover 40 miles from Fort Ticonderoga to Saratoga, and lost hundreds of men to American snipers.

127

GRAPHIC ORGANIZERS

As you read and study history, geography, and the social sciences, you'll start to collect a lot of information. Using a graphic organizer is one way to make information clearer and easier to understand. You can choose from different types of organizers, depending on the information.

OUTLINE

MAIN IDEA: _____

DETAIL: _____

DETAIL: _____

DETAIL: _____

MAIN IDEA: _____

DETAIL: _____

DETAIL: _____

DETAIL: _____

Outline

To build an outline, first identify your main idea. Write this at the top. Then, in the lines below, list the details that support the main idea. Keep adding main ideas and details as you need to.

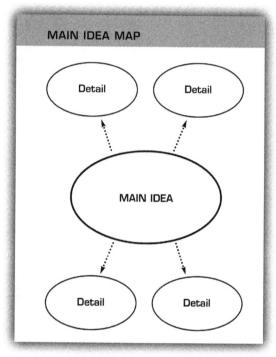

MAIN IDEA MAP

Main Idea Map

Write down your main idea in the central circle. Write details in the connecting circles.

K-W-L CHART

K	W	L
What I Know	What I Want to Know	What I Learned

K-W-L Chart

Before you read a chapter, write down what you already know about a subject in the left column. Then write what you want to know in the center column. Then write what you learned in the last column. You can make a two-column version of this. Write what you know in the left and what you learned after reading the chapter.

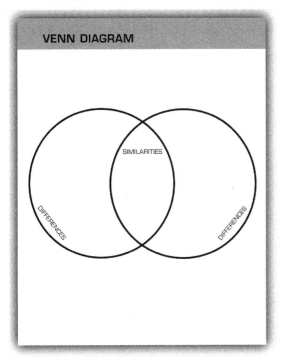

Venn Diagram

These overlapping circles show differences and similarities among topics. Each topic is shown as a circle. Any details the topics have in common go in the areas where those circles overlap. List the differences where the circles do not overlap.

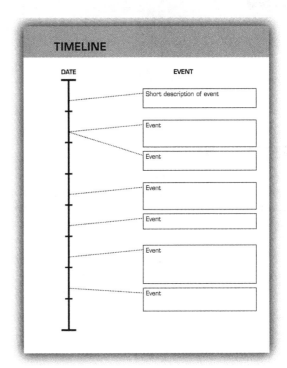

Timeline

A timeline divides a time period into equal chunks of time. Then it shows when events happened during that time. Decide how to divide up the timeline. Then write events in the boxes to the right when they happened. Connect them to the date line.

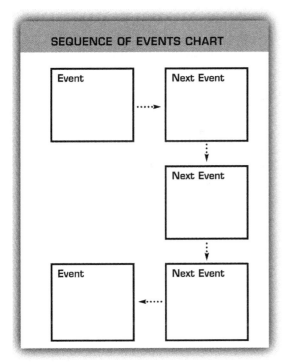

Sequence of Events Chart

Historical events bring about changes. These result in other events and changes. A sequence of events chart uses linked boxes to show how one event leads to another, and then another.

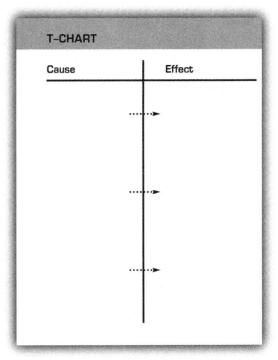

T-Chart

Use this chart to separate information into two columns. To separate causes and effects, list events, or causes, in one column. In the other column, list the change, or effect, each event brought about.

REPORTS AND SPECIAL PROJECTS

Aside from the activities in this Study Guide, your teacher may ask you to do some extra research or reading about American history on your own. Or, you might become interested in a particular story you read in *A History of US* and want to find out more. Do you know where to start?

GETTING STARTED

The back of every History of US book has a section called "More Books to Read." Some of these books are fiction and some are nonfiction. This list is different for each book in the series. When you want to find out more about a particular topic from the reading, these books are a great place to start—and you should be able to find all of them in your school library.

Also, if you're specifically looking for *primary sources*, you can start with the *History of US Sourcebook and Index*. This book is full of *primary sources*, words and evidence about history directly from the people who were involved. This is an excellent place to find the exact words from important speeches and documents.

DOING RESEARCH

For some of the group projects and assignments in this course, you will need to conduct research either in a library or online. When your teacher asks you to research a topic, remember the following tips:

TO FIND GOOD EVIDENCE, START WITH GOOD SOURCES

Usually, your teacher will expect you to support your research with *primary sources*. Remember that a primary source for an event comes from someone who was there when the event took place. The best evidence for projects and writing assignments always comes from *primary sources*, so if you can't seem to find any right away, keep looking.

ASK THE LIBRARIAN

Librarians are amazing people who can help you find just about anything in the library. If you can't seem to find what you're looking for, remember to ask a librarian for help.

WHEN RESEARCHING ONLINE, STICK TO CREDIBLE WEBSITES

It can be difficult to decide which websites are credible and which are not. To be safe, stick with websites that both you and your teacher trust. There are plenty of online sources that have information you can trust to be correct, and usually they're names you already know. For example, you can trust the facts you get from places like pbs.org, census.gov, historychannel.com, and historyofus.com. In addition to free websites like these, check with your librarian to see which *databases and subscription-based websites* your school can access.

USE THE LIBRARY/MEDIA CENTER RESEARCH LOG

At the back of this study guide, you'll find several copies of a Library/Media Center Research Log. Take one with you to the library or media center, and keep track of your sources. Also, take time to decide how helpful and relevant those sources are.

OTHER RESOURCES

Your school and public library have lots of additional resources to help you with your research. These include videos, DVDs, software, and CDs.

CHAPTER 1

FREEDOM OF THE PRESS

SUMMARY *The trial of Peter Zenger galvanized the colonists and laid the foundation for two fundamental principles of liberty in America: freedom of the press and trial by jury.*

ACCESS

This chapter introduces one of the most important trials in American history. To trace the events, use your history journal to make a sequence of events chart in like the one on page 9 of this study guide. In the first box of your chart, write *Lawyers urge Peter Zenger to start a newspaper.* In the last box, write *Jury finds Zenger not guilty.* Put at least five entries between the first and last boxes.

WORD BANK   apprentice   disbarred   arbitrary   indentured servant   libel   bribes

Choose words from the word bank to complete the sentences below. One word is not used at all.

1. An _____ decision is made without asking for other opinions.

2. An _____ worked for the person who paid for his or her voyage to the colonies.

3. A lawyer who is _____ cannot practice law.

4. An _____ had a chance to learn a trade.

5. A person who publishes something false and harmful about another person can be tried for

_____ .

WORD PLAY

In a dictionary, look up the word that was not used. Rewrite the sentence in the chapter in which the word appears, using the definition.

CRITICAL THINKING   MAKING INFERENCES

Some of the statements below could have been made by the attorney general in Zenger's trial. Others sound like something the defense might have said. Mark the statements *AG* for attorney general or *D* for the defense.

_____ 1. Truth is no defense against a charge of libel.

_____ 2. The governor has special rights, just like a king.

_____ 3. Free men have a right to express their opinions.

_____ 4. Truth is a defense against a charge of libel.

_____ 5. A jury cannot decide innocence or guilt.

_____ 6. Juries have the right to decide innocence or guilt.

WORKING WITH PRIMARY SOURCES

Read the words of Gouverneur Morris below.

> The trial of Zenger in 1735 was the germ of American freedom, the morning star of that liberty which subsequently revolutionized America.

Rewrite Morris's opinion about the Zenger case in your own words in your history journal.

WRITING

Imagine you are reading the newspaper in 1735, when Peter Zenger won his case. In your history journal, write a headline that might have appeared in the *New York Gazette* .Then, write a headline that might have appeared in Zenger's own paper, *The New York Weekly Journal.*

JENKINS' EAR

SUMMARY *When the Spaniards cut off Jenkins' ear, war was the result. The issue was not Jenkins' ear but control of North America.*

ACCESS

This chapter discusses a little-known war in which colonial fighters were first called "Americans." In your history journal, make a three-column chart. Label the columns *Wars*, *Combatants* and *Causes and Results*. As you read, fill in the chart with information you find.

WORD BANK   people's war

Find the term above on page 17. Write the sentence that defines the term on the line below.

_____

CRITICAL THINKING FACT OR OPINION

A fact is a statement that can be proven. An opinion is a belief that may or may not be true. Label each sentence below F or O.

_____ 1. I want to tell you about the War of Jenkins' Ear, partly because of that ridiculous name, but also because it was

   interesting.

_____ 2. The fighting went on for nine years, with naval battles from North Carolina to Colombia in South America.

_____ 3. For the first time, colonial troops were officially called "Americans" by the English, instead of "provincials" or

   "colonials."

_____ 4. Captain Lawrence Washington, George's half brother, was one of those who fought in the war.

_____ 5. Something else came from that war, something silly.

WORKING WITH PRIMARY SOURCES

Read the agreement between Lawrence Washington's widow, Ann Lee, and George Washington about Mount Vernon. In your history journal, answer the questions that follow with complete sentences.

> George Washington [will] pay yearly . . . unto Ann Lee . . . fifteen thousand pounds of tobacco . . . or as much Current money . . . as will be equal there to at twelve shillings . . . for every hundred [pounds] of tobacco . . . the first rent . . . due on the twenty-fifth day of December.

1 What did George Washington have to do each year to live in Mount Vernon?

2. On page 17, the author says that a shilling was worth about 7 1/2 cents. How much was one hundred pounds of

   tobacco worth?

3. How much was the entire crop of tobacco worth that Washington had to pay?

4. What is unusual about the day the payment was due each year?

FRENCHMEN AND INDIANS

SUMMARY *The French and Indian War determined the future of the continent. It also taught colonial leaders, such as George Washington, valuable lessons that would later help them shake off British rule.*

ACCESS

In chapter 3, you read about many similarities and differences between the French and English strategies in North America. To help organize these similarities and differences, copy the Venn diagram from page 9 into your history journal, and label one circle *French* and the other *English*. As you read the chapter, fill in the circles with facts about the two nations.

WORD BANK   frontier   surveyor   musket   drain

Complete the sentences below with words from the word bank. One word is not used.

1. The "Brown Bess" was a _____ that was used by British troops.

2. English settlers moved west to the _____ as the coast became more populated.

3. A _____ mapped and measured land.

WITH A PARENT OR PARTNER

Discuss the following questions with a parent or partner. Write your answers in your history journal.

1. Do any place names near your town come from Indian words?

2. Look up the name of the original Native American tribe or tribes that lived in your area.

3. Who were the first European settlers to come to the area?

CRITICAL THINKING SEQUENCE OF EVENTS

The sentences below describe events in the first years of the French and Indian War. Put them in sequence by writing numbers in the blanks next to each event. (Write "1" next to the earliest event, and so forth.)

_____ Washington and his men were defeated by the French at Fort Necessity.

_____ The French built Fort Duquesne to protect their claim to the Ohio River Valley.

_____ French and Indian forces, hidden in the forests, destroyed English forces.

_____ General Braddock led British troops against Fort Duquesne.

_____ Washington was sent to Fort Duquesne by the British to order the French to leave the Ohio River Valley.

WORKING WITH PRIMARY SOURCES

Read the words of Braddock and Washington below. In your history journal, answer the questions that follow.

> We are sent like lambs to slaughter. —Major General Edward Braddock
> [Soldiers] broke and ran as sheep pursued by dogs. —George Washington

1. Who will "slaughter" Braddock's troops?

2. Who are the "dogs" that pursue Washington's troops?_

3. Why do you think Braddock and Washington used the words "lambs" and "sheep" to describe the men under their

command?

WRITING

Read the description of the Brown Bess on page 24. Imagine you are a gun shop owner from colonial America. In your history journal, make a poster advertising the Brown Bess. Be sure to illustrate for interested soldiers how the Brown Bess works, and show its internal parts.

CHAPTER 4

A MOST REMARKABLE MAN

SUMMARY *An amazing English/Mohawk American named Warraghiyagey (William Johnson) helped change the course of the French and Indian War in favor of the British. Contact with the Iroquois League also fueled visions of union in the minds of colonists such as Ben Franklin.*

ACCESS

To help you understand the importance of William Johnson's relationship with the Indians, make a K-W-L graphic organizer in your history journal like the one on page 8 of this study guide. In the "What I *Know*" column, write what you know about the Indians during the French and Indian War. Then, skim through the chapter, looking at illustrations and maps, and think of what you'd like to find out. In the "What I *Want* to Know" column, write five questions you have about the Indians. After you read the chapter, fill in the "What I *Learned*" column with answers to your questions and other information.

WORD BANK   feudal lord   sachem   baronet   ally

Complete the sentences below with words from the word bank. One word is not used.

1. A _____ was also called a knight or a nobleman.

2. A _____ was an Indian leader.

3. A _____ was a wealthy landowner.

CRITICAL THINKING   DRAWING CONCLUSIONS

Each of the sentences in *italics* below is taken from the chapter. Put a check mark in front of all of the conclusions that can be drawn from reading the lines.

1. *Johnson soon learned the ways of the Mohawk and was named as one of them.*

____ (a) Johnson admired Indian society.

____ (b) Mohawks trusted Johnson.

____ (c) Johnson gave his lands to the Mohawk.

2. *The Iroquois had united six tribes into a confederation.*

____ (a) The Iroquois were a powerful tribe.

____ (b) The French feared the Iroquois.

____ (c) In a confederation, different groups join together for protection.

3. *The small army of Native Americans and American colonists beat the French—all by themselves, without the aid of the regular British army.*

____ (a) The French did not have Indian allies.

____ (b) The American colonists were ruled by England.

____ (c) The British army was a powerful fighting force.

WORKING WITH PRIMARY SOURCES

Read the words of a Massachusetts doctor about William Johnson. In your history journal, write complete sentences to answer the questions.

> A gentleman of uncommon smart sense and even temper . . . he is almost universally beloved . . . for coolness of head and warmness of heart.

1. In the statement, is "temper" a good thing or a bad thing? Explain. What other word could be used instead of temper?

2. What does the expression "coolness of head" mean?

3. What does the expression "warmness of heart" mean?

4. Rewrite the statement about William Johnson from the last exercise using modern language.

CHAPTER 5

PITT STEPS IN

SUMMARY *With the help of the colonists and their Native American allies, the British won the French and Indian War. However, another conflict soon arose over who should pay for the war.*

ACCESS

Make a timeline like the one on page 9 of this study guide in your history journal with the dates and events on page 33. Label it to show the outcome of different battles and the end of the French and Indian War.

WORD BANK   foreign secretary   diplomat   treaty

Complete the sentences below with words from the word bank. One word is not used.

1. A _____ leads his or her country in relations with other countries.

2. A _____ represents his or her country in meetings with other countries.

MAP

Study the map on page 33. Then answer the the questions below.

1. French supplies for Fort Duquesne traveled from Quebec down the _____ River to Lake _____ and Lake _____.
   - (a) Hudson, George, Erie
   - (b) St. Lawrence, Ontario, Erie

2. Fort Niagara was located between Lake _____ and Lake _____.
   - (a) George, Ontario
   - (b) Erie, George
   - (c) Ontario, Erie

3. British troops landing in New York would travel _____ on the _____ River to reach Albany.
   - (a) west, Ohio
   - (b) east, St. Lawrence
   - (c) north, Hudson

4. The British capture of _____ prevented French troops and supplies from entering the _____ River.
   - (a) Louisbourg, St. Lawrence
   - (b) Montreal, St. Lawrence

WORKING WITH PRIMARY SOURCES

Read this description of the Battle of Quebec, written by a soldier who fought for the British. In your history journal, answer the questions that follow.

> [French] Regulars then . . . gave us their first fire, at about fifty yards distance, which we did not return, as it was General Wolfe's express orders not to fire till they came within twenty yards of us —They continued firing . . . advancing . . . till they came close up to us, and then the Action became general: In about a quarter of an hour the enemy gave way . . . when a terrible slaughter ensued from the quick fire of our field pieces and muskets.

1. How far away from the British lines were the French when they opened fire?

2. Why didn't the British return fire?

3. About how long did this part of the battle last?

4. In which previous chapter have you read the word "slaughter?" Who said it, and what was the situation?

AU REVOIR (GOODBYE), FRANCE

SUMMARY *The spoils of war went to Great Britain. For their support, the Iroquois got nothing. Worse yet, land-hungry colonists cast their eyes on Indian territory west of the Appalachians.*

ACCESS

This chapter is a summary of the results of the French and Indian War. A good graphic organizer to use is the main idea map on page 8 of this study guide. Copy the diagram into your history journal. In the largest circle, write the words *French and Indian War.* Fill in each of the webs with facts about war's outcome.

WORD BANK   territory   presidio   mission

Complete the sentences below with words from the word bank. One word is not used.

1. A _____ was a Spanish settlement around a church.

2. A _____ was a fort that protected Spanish settlers.

WORD PLAY

Look up the remaining word in a dictionary. Then find a sentence in chapter 6 that contains that word. Rewrite the sentence using the definition in place of the word itself.

_____

WORKING WITH PRIMARY SOURCES

Read these words from a letter written by Lord Jeffrey Amherst to an English officer regarding the Indians. In your history journal, answer the questions that follow.

> We must . . . use every stratagem in our power to reduce them. You will therefore take no prisoners, but put to death all that fall into your hands . . . [W]hen a native is captured he is to . . . immediately be put to death, their extirpation being the only security for our future safety.

1. In the statement, what does the word "reduce" mean? What other word could be used instead of reduce?

2. What does Amherst say should be done with captured Indians?

3. From the passage, can you figure out what "extirpation" means? Use a dictionary to check the meaning.

"Extirpation" and "reduce" as used here are *euphemisms*, mild expressions used instead of others that could seem too harsh. With a parent or partner, brainstorm a list of common euphemisms and write them in your history journal. Write down situations where euphemisms could help or hurt. Explain your point of view.

STAYING IN CHARGE

SUMMARY *Great Britain tried to control the westward movement of colonists with the Proclamation of 1763. But independent-minded pioneers like Daniel Boone had no intention of following orders from faraway England.*

ACCESS

This chapter discusses the results of the British victory in the French and Indian War. In your history journal, make a cause and effect chart like the one on page 9 of this study guide. For the first cause, write *England had to keep the English colonists and the Native Americans from killing each other*. List the effect. Fill in at four other cause-and-effect relationships from the chapter as you read.

WORD BANK   Great Awakening   proclamation   speculator

Underline the root words in *awakening*, *proclamation*, and *speculator*. In your history journal, write a sentence using the root word of each.

MAP

Use the map on page 37 to answer these questions.

1. The Ohio River flowed _____ of the Proclamation Line of 1763.

_____ (a) east _____ (b) south _____ (c) west

2. Any settlers who traveled the Ohio River to find land were _____ the king's proclamation.

____ (a) obeying _____ (b) ignoring _____ (c) extending

3. The Indian reserve was located _____ of the Mississippi River.

___ (a) east _____ (b) west _____ (c) south

4. From studying the map, why do you think Fort Pitt was called "The Gateway to the West"?

WORKING WITH PRIMARY SOURCES

Read the words of Daniel Boone below. In your history journal, answer the questions that follow.

> It was on the first of May 1769, that I resigned my domestic happiness, and left my family and peaceable habitation . . . to wander through the wilderness of America, in quest of the country of Kentucke.

1. What is another way to say "I resigned my domestic happiness"?

2. What is another word for "habitation"?

3. Which direction do you think Boone planned to "wander through the wilderness"?

4. Why did Boone leave home?

WRITING

Imagine that you are about to set off with Daniel Boone on his "quest." In your history journal, write a short goodbye note to your family. Illustrate it with pictures or cartoons.

WHAT IS AN AMERICAN?

SUMMARY *Even before the Revolution, Hector St. John Crèvecœur sensed the creation of a new people called "Americans." Their society blended English liberty with a sense of freedom and opportunity that came from having a vast frontier.*

ACCESS

This chapter discusses a famous book that describes an early definition of the word "American." A good graphic organizer for this chapter is the main idea map on page 8 of this study guide. Copy the diagram into your history journal. In the largest circle, write *American*. Fill in the connecting circles with words that Crèvecœur used to describe Americans.

WORD BANK   yeoman (YO-man) farmers   posterity

Find the terms above in this chapter. Use a dictionary to look up the one that is not defined in the text. Then rewrite the sentences using the definitions in place of the terms themselves. (Hint: One term is found in the original writing of Crèvecœur.)

1. _____

2. _____

WITH A PARENT OR PARTNER

Think about the question that is asked by this chapter's title. Brainstorm five or six things that you think define an American.

CRITICAL THINKING FACT OR OPINION

A fact is a statement that can be proven. An opinion is a belief that may or may not be true. Label each sentence below F or O.

_____ 1. Crèvecœur was a mapmaker for General Montcalm.

_____ 2. "The American is a new man, who acts upon new principles."

_____ 3. "We are the most perfect society now existing in the world."

_____ 4. American laws, he said, let people think for themselves.

_____ 5. Most Americans didn't like societies that kept rich and poor apart.

_____ 6. When he came back to America his wife was dead, his house was burned, and his two younger children were gone.

WORKING WITH PRIMARY SOURCES

Read Crèvecœur's words below. In your history journal, answer the questions that follow.

> The American is a new man, who acts upon new principles; he must therefore entertain new ideas and form new opinions.

1. Crèvecœur wrote about four "new" things in the passage above: *new man, new principles, new ideas,* and *new opinions.* Think about what he was referring to with each phrase. How, or in what way, was each thing new? Brainstorm possible ideas and make notes under each of these four headings.

2. Then, rewrite the passage as a paragraph, using your own words and the notes you wrote.

3. Do you think Crèvecœur's description is still true today? Why or why not?

CHAPTER 9

A GIRL WHO ALWAYS DID HER BEST

SUMMARY *Eliza Lucas showed how the colonial experience changed the world. In an era when women had few rights, Eliza carved out a role as a scientist and business manager.*

ACCESS

Make a graphic organizer in your history journal like the one on page 8 of this study guide. In the "What I *Know*" column, write what you know about colonial farming (check chapter 8). Then, skim through the chapter, looking at illustrations and maps, and think of what you'd like to find out. In the "What I *Want* to Know" column, write five questions you have about a "girl" running a plantation. After you read the chapter, fill out the "What I *Learned*" column with answers to your questions and other information.

WORD BANK   indigo   Founding Mother

Answer the questions below with complete sentences.

1. What sentence on page 44 explains the meaning of "Founding Mother"?

_____

2. What sentence on page 43 explains why Eliza grew indigo?

_____

CRITICAL THINKING   DRAWING CONCLUSIONS

Each of the sentences in *italics* below is taken from the chapter. Put a check mark in front of all of the conclusions that can be drawn from reading the lines.

1. *Eliza Lucas was one of those from the privileged plantation world.*

_____ (a) Eliza Lucas came from a wealthy family.

_____ (b) Eliza Lucas was against slavery.

_____ (c) Eliza Lucas grew up in the country rather than the city.

2. *In 1744, Eliza Lucas grew the first successful indigo crop in the colonies.*

_____ (a) Other planters had tried and failed to grow indigo.

_____ (b) Eliza actually planted and harvested the indigo in the fields.

_____ (c) Eliza understood agriculture and plant life.

3. *She was training the girls to teach the other slave children—and that was very unusual in Eliza's day.*

_____ (a) Women were not allowed to go to school in colonial times.

_____ (b) Slave children were not educated in colonial times.

_____ (c) Eliza believed that education was important for all children.

WORKING WITH PRIMARY SOURCES

Read the words of Eliza Lucas below, written when she was a teenager. In your history journal, answer the questions that follow.

> I have the business of three plantations to transact . . . [which] requires much writing and more business and fatigue of other sorts than you can imagine.

1. What is another way to say "I have the business of three plantations to transact"?
2. What kind of writing do you think Eliza had to do to run a plantation?
3. Why do you think Eliza said there was more "fatigue of other sorts than you can imagine"?

WRITING

In your history journal, make a list of all of the jobs that you think Eliza took care of in her role. Try to think of at least five. Imagine you were Eliza. Arrange the jobs in order from least favorite to most favorite, with reasons for your choice. Make drawings or cut pictures out or a magazine to illustrate your list.

THE RIGHTS OF ENGLISHMEN

SUMMARY *English settlers were no strangers to conflict in the name of liberty. The cornerstones of English government were forged out of conflicts between the English people and their rulers.*

ACCESS

This chapter introduces you to three important historical events in England that led to the Declaration of Independence and the United States Constitution. To help organize the information in the chapter, make an outline with three sections like the one on page 8 of this study guide, in your history journal. Label the sections *Magna Carta*, *habeas corpus*, and *Glorious Revolution*. As you read, fill in facts for each section.

WORD BANK

Glorious Revolution   Magna Carta   Bill of Rights
writ of habeas corpus   constitution

In your history journal, write a short paragraph that includes all the terms in the word bank.

CRITICAL THINKING   SEQUENCE OF EVENTS

Label the following events "B" if they took place before the Magna Carta was signed or "A" if they took place after the Magna Carta was signed.

_____ 1. The Pope closed all the churches in England.

_____ 2. King William and Queen Mary signed a Bill of Rights.

_____ 3. People were put in jail and not told the reason for their arrest.

_____ 4. King John took land and money from the barons.

_____ 5. A person could not be put in jail without a fair trial by his peers.

_____ 6. King John was imprisoned on the island of Runnymede.

_____ 7. A person's words could not be used against him in court.

_____ 8. The Declaration of Independence and the U.S. Constitution were written.

WORKING WITH PRIMARY SOURCES

A *ballad* is a simple, poetic song that tells a story. Read the ballad from page 46 below and answer the questions that follow in your history journal.

> An ancient story I'll tell you anon,
> Of a notable prince, that was called King John
> He ruled over England with main and might,
> But he did great wrong, and maintained little right.

1. How do you know that ballad was written long after King John's reign had ended?

2. What is another word for "might"?

3. What is the writer's opinion of King John?

CHAPTER 11

A TAXING KING

SUMMARY *The British tried to raise taxes on tea, every kind of printed matter, and a variety of other goods. Instead of paying the taxes willingly, the colonists sent the British a message: "No taxation without representation."*

ACCESS

This chapter discusses the main reasons that the colonists rebelled against England. To organize the information, copy the main idea map from page 8 of this study guide into your history journal. In the big circle, write *Taxes*. In the smaller circles, list the details from the chapter.

WORD BANK   Stamp Act   repeal

Look for a *description* of the first term, "Stamp Act," on page 53 of your book. Look for a *definition* of the word "repeal" on the same page. Write a sentence using both the description and the definition, but without using either word.

WORKING WITH PRIMARY SOURCES

Read what George Hewes says about the Boston Tea Party. In your history journal, answer the questions below.

> We then were ordered by our commander to . . . take out all the chests of tea and throw them overboard, and we immediately proceeded to execute his order. First cutting and splitting the chests with our tomahawks, so as to thoroughly expose them to the effects of water.

1. Imagine you are a reporter for a London newspaper. What headline would you write for the event that George Hewes describes?

2. Now imagine that you write for a Boston newspaper. What headline would you write?

3. Choose one of the newspapers and write news article about the event based on your "interview" with George Hewes and other information you have learned from the chapter. Write at least one paragraph in your history journal.

WRITING

How would you design a stamp that commemorates the repeal of the Stamp Act? In your history journal, draw a poster-size version of a stamp that describes the colonists' feelings about the Stamp Act.

HISTORY JOURNAL

Don't forget to share your history journal with your classmates, and ask if you can see what their journals look like. You might be surprised—and get some new ideas.

THE FIREBRANDS

SUMMARY *Three firebrands helped spark the American Revolution with their actions and words. From north to south, people soon knew the names Samuel Adams, Thomas Paine, and Patrick Henry.*

ACCESS

To help understand the importance of Samuel Adams, Thomas Paine, and Patrick Henry, make a K-W-L graphic organizer in your history journal like the one on page 8 of this study guide. In the "What I *Know*" column, write what you know about these firebrands. (If you don't know anything, just write their names.) Then, skim through the chapter, looking at illustrations and maps, and think of what you'd like to find out. In the "What I *Want* to Know" column, write three questions you have about each man. After you read the chapter, fill in the "What I *Learned*" column with answers to your questions and other information.

WORD BANK

firebrand   committee of correspondence   deist   burgesses

Complete the sentences below with words from the word bank. One word is not used.

1. A _____ is someone who has strong beliefs in a higher power.

2. A _____ is someone who had strong beliefs about government power.

3. The _____ was a group that communicated political information between the colonies.

CRITICAL THINKING   DRAWING CONCLUSIONS

Put an "A" in front of the sentences below that refer to Samuel Adams. Put an "H" in front of the sentences that refer to Patrick Henry. Put a "P" in front of the sentences that refer to Thomas Paine.

_____ 1. Arrived in Philadelphia from London half dead from a fever.

_____ 2. Was a planter and storekeeper before he studied law.

_____ 3. Served in Virginia's House of Burgesses.

_____ 4. Helped to organize the Boston Tea Party.

_____ 5. Lost much of the family money as a failed businessman in Boston.

_____ 6. Got a job on a magazine, thanks to a letter from Benjamin Franklin.

_____ 7. Said, "Give me liberty or give me death."

_____ 8. Wrote a pamphlet entitled "Common Sense."

WORKING WITH PRIMARY SOURCES

Read this passage written by Thomas Paine. In your history journal, answer the questions that follow.

> These are the times that try men's souls: The summer soldier and the sunshine patriot will, in this crisis, shrink from the service of his country; but he that stands it now, deserves the love and thanks of man and woman.

1. Does Paine like or dislike "summer" soldiers and "sunshine" patriots? Explain.

2. What "country" is Paine referring to?

IN YOUR OWN WORDS

Take another look at Thomas Paine's quote in the last exercise. Restate his point, using your own words, in your history journal.

A MASSACRE IN BOSTON

SUMMARY *The Boston Massacre highlighted the rabble-rousing that fueled revolutionary feeling. The conduct of John Adams in the trial that followed and the weighty questions considered by the Continental Congress showed the caliber of the colonial leaders.*

ACCESS

This chapter describes the events of the early 1770s that led to revolution. The most important such event was the *Boston Massacre*. In your history journal, make a cause and effect T-chart like the one on page 9 of this study guide. For the first cause, write *British troops are quartered in Boston*. List the effect. Fill in at least four more cause-and-effect relationships.

WORD BANK

| Quartering Act | redcoats | militia | deserters | Boston Massacre |
| Continental Congress | | propaganda | | |

Complete the sentences below with words from the word bank. One word is not used.

1. The _____ forced the people of Boston to provide housing for _____.

2. Delegates at the _____ advised each colony to raise and arm a _____.

3. Soldiers who run away from army duty are called _____.

4. The _____ was exaggerated by Samuel Adams and Paul Revere.

CRITICAL THINKING SEQUENCE OF EVENTS

The sentences below describe events from 1765 to 1774. Put them in order by writing numbers in the blanks next to each event. (Write "1" next to the earliest event, and so forth.)

____ The Continental Congress meets in Philadelphia.

____ Redcoats open fire on a group of colonial troublemakers in Boston.

____ Parliament passes the Quartering Law.

____ John Adams defends British soldiers charged with murder.

____ British soldiers arrive in Boston from England.

____ Delegates write a petition to King George.

____ Paul Revere makes an engraving of the "Boston Massacre."

____ A jury in Boston finds the redcoats not guilty of murder.

WORKING WITH PRIMARY SOURCES

Read the words of John Adams below, spoken during his defense of the British soldiers. In your history journal, answer the questions that follow.

> Facts are stubborn things; and whatever may be our wishes, our inclinations, or the dictates of our passion, they cannot alter the . . . facts and evidence.

1. To whom do you think Adams was speaking?

2. What might be the wishes of the people to whom he is speaking?

3. Why does Adams call facts "stubborn things"?

WRITING

A storyboard is a collection of pictures that show an action, like a comic strip. A storyboard can contain drawing, collage, or photos. Read the description of the Boston Massacre on pages 64-65. Then, in your history journal, make a storyboard retelling what happened.

CHAPTER 14

ONE IF BY LAND, TWO IF BY SEA

SUMMARY *Conflict turned to war when the minutemen and redcoats scuffled at Lexington and Concord. The march toward nationhood had begun.*

ACCESS

This chapter described the first battle of the American Revolution. Copy a sequence of events graphic organizer, like the one shown on page 9 of this study guide, into your history journal. In the first box, write *British cross Boston Harbor and march to Lexington*. Fill in at least five boxes with events that follow.

WORD BANK   patriot   loyalist   minuteman   traitor

Complete the sentences below with words from the word bank. One word is not used.

1. A _____ would fight as a _____ and would consider a _____ his enemy.

CRITICAL THINKING   MAKING INFERENCES

Put a "P" in front of the sentences below that describe events from the point of view of a patriot. Put a "B" in front of the sentences that describe events from the British point of view.

_____ 1. "The redcoats are coming."

_____ 2. "Disperse you rebels . . . thrown down your arms and disperse."

_____ 3. "But if they mean to have a war, let it begin here!"

_____ 4. "And several guns were fired upon the King's troops from behind a stone wall."

_____ 5. "I haven't a man who is afraid to go."

_____ 6. "In consequence of this attack by the rebels, the troops returned fire and killed several of them."

_____ 7. "Eight of our men were killed and nine wounded."

_____ 8. "Six companies of light infantry . . . at Lexington found a body of the country people under arms."

WORKING WITH PRIMARY SOURCES

Read the words of Isaac Davis's wife. In your history journal, answer the questions that follow.

Isaac Davis . . . said but little that morning. He seemed serious and thoughtful, but never seemed to hesitate . . . He only said "take good care of the children." In the afternoon he was brought home a corpse.

1. What happened to Isaac Davis?

2. Besides "serious" and "thoughtful," what other words do you think could be used to describe Davis?

WRITING

Imagine that you are writing the obituary—death notice—for Isaac Davis in the *Lexington and Concord Gazette*. In your history journal, describe the events surrounding Davis's death and mention the family he leaves behind. Make sure to give the date of his death: April 19, 1775.

AN AMERICAN ORIGINAL

SUMMARY *The British possessed battle-tested generals. But the colonists boasted the raw courage of backwoods fighters such as Ethan Allen, who proved his daring with the capture of Fort Ticonderoga.*

ACCESS

Copy the cause and effect chart from page 9 of this study guide into your history journal. Tell the story of Ethan Allen as a series of cause-and-effect statements. For the first cause, write: *He was asked to leave his hometown.* What was the effect? List at least four more cause-and-effect statements.

MAP

Compare the map on page 77 of your book with a modern map of New England and New York.

1. What is the name of the river that flows through Massachusetts and Connecticut? _____

2. What colonial capital is missing from the map? (Hint: It's the capital of Connecticut.) _____

3. Where is the border of the modern state of Vermont? _____

WORD BANK   Green Mountain Boys   Enlightenment

Find the paragraph on page 76 of your book that discusses the Green Mountain Boys. List three facts about the group.

1. _____

2. _____

3. _____

Find the paragraph on page 79 of your book that describes the time period known as the Enlightenment. List three facts about that time period.

1. _____

2. _____

3. _____

WORKING WITH PRIMARY SOURCES

Read these words about Americans from an article written in England around 1776. In your history journal, write complete sentences to answer the questions.

> The darling passion of the American is liberty . . . nor is it the original natives only to whom this passion is confined, our colonists sent thither seem to have imbibed the same principles.

1. What is another way to say "darling passion"?

2. What does the term "original natives" mean?

3. What is another way to say "our colonists sent thither"?

4. What is another word for "imbibed?" (Look it up in the dictionary if you don't know.)

WRITING

Rewrite the statement about the colonists' "darling passion" for "liberty" in modern language in your history journal.

ON THE WAY TO THE SECOND CONTINENTAL CONGRESS

SUMMARY *Few of the delegates who traveled to Philadelphia in 1775 wanted to rush headlong into revolution. However, with bullets flying in Boston, most wondered how long they could continue to call themselves English subjects.*

ACCESS

This chapter introduces the men who were delegates to the Second Continental Congress. Copy the main idea map from page 8 of this study guide into your history journal. In the large circle, write *Delegates Philadelphia 1775*. In the smaller circles, write the names of delegates, the colonies they represented, and any other facts.

WORD BANK   legislative authority   commonwealth   orators

Complete the sentences below with words from the word bank. One word is not used.

1. A law passed by _____ is voted on by elected officials.

2. The colony of Virginia was known as a _____.

CRITICAL THINKING   FACT OR OPINION

A fact is a statement that can be proven. An opinion is a belief that may or may not be true. Label each sentence below F or O.

_____ 1. He wore his military uniform to Philadelphia—bright blue with brass buttons—and they called him Colonel
Washington.

_____ 2. John Adams was always jealous of George Washington.

_____ 3. As Lee and Washington rode towards Philadelphia, they were joined by other members of the Virginia
delegation.

_____ 4. Three were the best orators in the state, perhaps in the nation.

_____ 5. In June Franklin was back at the Convention, where he was asked to serve (with John Adams and Thomas
Jefferson) on a committee that was to write an important document.

_____ 6. This was the most important political document ever written.

WORKING WITH PRIMARY SOURCES

Read John Adams's description of Caesar Rodney, the delegate from Delaware. In your history journal, answer the questions that follow.

> He is the oddest looking man in the world; his face is not bigger than a large apple, yet there is a sense of fire, spirit, wit, and humor in his countenance.

1. What, according to Adams, makes Rodney "the oddest looking man in the world"?

2. What is another word that has the same meaning as "fire" in this description?

3. How is "fire" different from "spirit"?

4. What is the difference between "wit" and "humor"?

WRITING

Choose one of the images in the chapter. In your history journal, write a description of that person. Compare his face to something in nature. Make your own picture, poster, or cartoon of the person.

NAMING A GENERAL

SUMMARY *The task of shaping a raggedy militia into a Continental army fell to George Washington. Rejection of the Olive Branch Petition by King George III helped ensure that Washington would remain on the battlefield for nearly six years.*

ACCESS

This chapter covers an important period of time in the early years of the American Revolution. Copy the timeline graphic organizer from page 9 of this study guide into your history journal. Next, enter the dates that are given in the right-hand column on page 85 of your book. Leave enough room to add to this timeline.

WORD BANK   Olive Branch Petition

Find a description of the above phrase in your book. List three facts that pertain to it.

1. _____

2. _____

3. _____

COMPREHENSION   MAIN IDEA AND SUPPORTING DETAILS

Each sentence in *italics* below states a main idea from the chapter. For each numbered sentence, put a check mark in the blank in front of the ONE statement that DOES NOT support, or tell more, about the main idea.

1. *In each of the colonies, citizen soldiers—militia—were ready to fight.*

___ (a) Someone had to organize the militia and the minutemen into an army.

___ (b) A general was needed, said Adams.

___ (c) In the meantime, the Continental Congress tried once more to patch things up with England.

2. *Washington knew that the general's job could lead to disaster.*

___ (a) England was the greatest power in the world.

___ (b) John Hancock from Massachusetts believed he was the man for the job.

___ (c) Its [England's] army was well trained and supplied with the latest guns and cannons.

3. *The colonists were petitioning England and at the same were getting ready to fight.*

___ (a) George Washington knew that he had an almost impossible job.

___ (b) But most members of the Congress weren't ready to break away from England.

___ (c) For a long time, many Americans thought they could have the rights of free people and still be part of the British empire.

WORKING WITH PRIMARY SOURCES

Read the words from the Olive Branch Petition below. In your history journal, answer the questions that follow.

> The apprehensions which now oppress our hearts with unspeakable grief, being once removed, your Majesty will find your faithful subjects on this continent . . . willing at all times . . . to assert the . . . interests of . . . our Mother country.

1. What is a modern way to say "apprehensions which now oppress our hearts"?

2. What are some "apprehensions" of the colonists?

3. How would these "apprehensions" be "removed"?

4. What is the "Mother country"?

WRITING

Imagine you are a newspaper editor in 1775. In your history journal, write a brief editorial in which you either agree or disagree with the Olive Branch Petition. (An editorial is different from a news story. It expresses the opinion of the editor or writer.)

THE WAR OF THE HILLS

SUMMARY *Battles at Breed's Hill and Bunker Hill introduced the redcoats to Patriot sharpshooters. The British forced the Patriots off the hills, but only at a terrible cost of life.*

ACCESS

To help understand the importance of the Battle of Bunker Hill, the chapter's topic, make a K-W-L graphic organizer in your history journal like the one on page 8 of this study guide. In the "What I *Know*" column, write what you know about the fighting between the colonists and the redcoats. Then, skim through the chapter, looking at illustrations and maps, and think of what you'd like to find out. In the "What I *Want* to Know" column, write five questions you have about the Battle of Bunker Hill. After you read the chapter, fill out the "What I *Learned*" column with answers to your questions and other information.

WORD BANK   fortifications   barracks   earthworks   bayonets   grapeshot

Complete the sentences below with words from the word bank. One word is not used.

1. The Patriots dug _____ to protect their position on Breed's Hill.

2. Blades attached to guns called _____ were the weapons most feared by the Patriots.

3. The sleeping quarters, or _____, of the British troops were built behind _____ in Boston.

CRITICAL THINKING   SEQUENCE OF EVENTS

The sentences below describe events in chapter 18. Put them in order by writing numbers in the blanks next to each event. (Write "1" next to the earliest event, and so forth.)

_____ 1. The British capture Breed's Hill and Bunker Hill.

_____ 2. The Continental Congress appoints George Washington commander of the Continental army.

_____ 3. Patriots begin to dig fortifications on Breed's Hill.

_____ 4. British soldiers rowed across Boston Harbor to Charlestown.

_____ 5. At dawn, Breed's Hill and Bunker Hill were controlled by Patriots.

_____ 6. Redcoats advance up the hill, bayonets pointed toward the enemy.

_____ 7. Bullets tore through the redcoats, leaving the hill covered in blood.

WORKING WITH PRIMARY SOURCES

Read the words of a Loyalist about Joseph Warren below. In your history journal, answer the questions that follow.

> Warren, a rascally patriot . . . was happily killed, in coming out of the trenches the other day . . .You may judge what the herd must be like when such a one is their leader.

1. How does the writer feel about Warren?

2. How does he describe Warren's death?

3. Who is the "herd" that the writer says the reader may "judge"?

4. What is the difference between what the writer thinks of the "herd" and what judgment Patriots would make about those who fought?

WRITING

In your history journal, draw the steps described in the Firing a Revolutionary Cannon feature on page 93. Create a series of drawings showing each step, showing a colonial soldier how to fire the cannon.

FIGHTING PALM TREES

SUMMARY *When British ships attacked Fort Sullivan in Charleston Harbor in South Carolina, it seemed that even the trees fought back. Cannonballs stuck in the fort's soft palmetto wood, while Patriot cannons blasted the British ships.*

ACCESS

Copy the sequence of events chart from page 9 of this guide into your history journal. The first event should be *British Navy sails to Charleston Harbor*. Fill in at least five more events from the information in the chapter.

WORD BANK   run aground   shoals

Find the paragraph on page 95 in which the terms above appear. Write a sentence using both of these terms. Then rewrite the sentence using the definitions of the terms.

1. _____

2. _____

MAP

Look at the map of the Revolutionary War battles in the Atlas section at the back of your back. Find the location of Charleston, South Carolina.

1. What colony is south of Charleston? _____

2. What do you think the weather is like there most of the time? _____

3. Why do you think that the fort on Sullivan Island was built with sand and palm trees? _____

WORKING WITH PRIMARY SOURCES

Read the lines from the poem below. In your history journal, answer the questions that follow.

> But, my lords, do not fear
> For before the next year,
> (Altho' a small island could fret us),
> The Continent whole
> We shall take, by my soul,
> If the cowardly Yankee will let us.

1. Who are the "lords" that the poet is speaking to?

2. What "small island" is the poet referring to?

3. What term does the poet use to refer to the Patriots?

WRITING

Write rhyming poem in your history journal to respond to the poem above. You can use some of these rhyming words or think up your own: *shoal, goal, hole; redcoat, afloat, small boat; coward, devoured, empowered; fear, steer, appear.*

DECLARING INDEPENDENCE

SUMMARY *The Declaration of Independence introduced the world to the American idea of democracy. Its lofty principles of equality and liberty have guided generations of Americans.*

SIGNING UP

SUMMARY *Today we call the delegates who signed the Declaration of Independence heroes. But King George III had another name for them—traitors.*

ACCESS

Find the exact wording for the Declaration of Independence in your book on page 190. Carefully read the first two sentences. These two sentences are very long. To help understand the wording in these sentences, break them up after every comma. Then, make a two column chart in your history journal. Rewrite the sentences in the left column of your chart, broken into phrases. In the right column, rewrite each phrase in your own words.

WORD BANK   declaration   consent of the governed

1. Find the root word of *declaration*. Write a sentence using that word.

_____

2. Look up the meaning of *consent* in a dictionary. Write a sentence explaining the meaning of the phrase "consent of the governed" that uses the definition you looked up.

_____

COMPREHENSION   WORDS IN CONTEXT

Examine these words taken from the Declaration of Independence. Mark the words that have the same meaning as the underlined word in the numbered phrases.

1. "We hold these Truths to be self-evident . . ."

    _____ (a) hidden   _____ (b) clear   _____ (c) selfish

2. "[T]hey are endowed by their Creator . . ."

    _____ (a) given   _____ (b) allowed   _____ (c) removed

3. "[W]ith certain unalienable rights . . ."

    ___ (a) temporary   _____ (b) foreign   ____ (c) absolute

4. "Governments are instituted among Men . . ."

    _____ (a) imprisoned   _____ (b) developed   _____ (c) overthrown

5. "[D]eriving their just powers . . ."

    ___ (a) receiving   ____ (b) criticizing   ____ (c) stealing

WORKING WITH PRIMARY SOURCES

Read the words of Benjamin Banneker below. In your history journal, answer the questions that follow.

> [O]ne universal Father hath given Being to us all, and that he hath . . . afforded us all the same sensations . . . the same faculties, and that however . . . diversified in situation or color, we are all of the same family . . .

1. What words does Banneker use that mean the same as Jefferson's word "Creator"?

2. What do you think Banneker means by the word "sensations"?

3. What do you think Banneker means by the term "faculties"?

4. What does the phrase "we are all of the same family" mean?

CHAPTER 22

REVOLUTIONARY WOMEN AND CHILDREN

SUMMARY *Women helped write the story of the Revolution. They served on the home front and the battlefront. The experience left many American women thirsting for greater equality.*

ACCESS

This chapter discusses the contributions and frustrations of women during the Revolution. To organize the information, copy the outline graphic organizer from page 8 of this study guide into your history journal. Title your outline *Revolutionary Women*. For main ideas write *Fighting*, *Rights* and *Disappointment*.

WORD BANK   hardtack   blockade   smallpox

Complete the sentences below with words from the word bank. One word is not used.

1. Women made _____ to feed the American troops.

2. A woman wrote a play about a _____ that kept food from reaching Boston.

Look up the remaining word in a dictionary. Find a sentence in chapter 22 that contains that word. Rewrite that sentence using the definition in place of the word itself.

_____

CRITICAL THINKING   FACT OR OPINION

A fact is a statement that can be proven. An opinion is a belief that may or may not be true. Label each sentence below F or O.

_____ 1. It was a war for a revolutionary idea: the idea that people could rule themselves.

_____ 2. Deborah Sampson disguised herself as a man.

_____ 3. A wife should have "good sense, a good disposition, a good reputation, and financial means."

_____ 4. "Even in their dresses the females seem to bid us defiance . . ."

_____ 5. "One word from her goes farther with [the Iroquois] than a thousand from any white man."

_____ 6. When it came to equality for women, Adams and the other delegates ignored the subject.

_____ 7. John Adams had no excuse at all for being obtuse on women's equality.

_____ 8. They couldn't vote.

_____ 9. "We have in common with all other men a natural right to our freedoms."

WORKING WITH PRIMARY SOURCES

Read the words of Abigail Adams below. In your history journal, answer the questions that follow.

In the new code of laws . . . remember the ladies . . . if particular care and attention are not paid . . . we are determined to foment a rebellion and will not hold ourselves bound to obey any laws in which we have no voice or representation.

1. Why is there a "new code of laws" being written at this time?

2. What does Adams mean by "particular care and attention"?

3. What is a modern way to say "will not hold ourselves bound"?

4. What is another way to say "no voice or representation"?

IN YOUR OWN WORDS

In your history journal, rewrite the warning from Abigail Adams above in modern language. Begin like this: "Before you put your John Hancock on any new laws, listen up!" Continue with at least three sentences.

23 FREEDOM FIGHTERS

SUMMARY *Perhaps nobody understood the limits on equality better than people of African ancestry. Some seized offers of freedom from the British. Others fought to plant the seeds of racial freedom in their own land.*

ACCESS

To help yourself understand the role played by African Americans in the Revolution, make a K-W-L graphic organizer in your history journal based on the one on page 8 of this study guide. In the "What I *Know*" column, write what you know about African Americans during the Revolution. Then, skim through the chapter, looking at illustrations and maps, and think of what you'd like to find out. In the "What I *Want* to Know" column, write five questions you have about the lives of African Americans during that time. After you read the chapter, fill out the "What I *Learned*" column with answers to your questions and other information about African Americans.

WORD BANK   privateer   powder boy (monkey)   pueblo   friar

Complete the sentences below with words from the word bank. One word is not used.

1. A _____ was an important crew member on a _____.

2. Explorers in the Southwest discovered an old _____ that had fallen to ruins.

CRITICAL THINKING SEQUENCE OF EVENTS

Label the following events "B" if they took place before James Forten was captured by the British or "A" if they took place after Forten was captured.

_____ 1. Forten spent seven months in a prison ship.

_____ 2. Forten learned to read and write.

_____ 3. Forten was a powder boy.

_____ 4. Forten helped found an antislavery society in Philadelphia.

_____ 5. Forten was a member of the crew of the Royal Louis when it captured a British ship.

_____ 6. Forten played marbles with a young English boy.

_____ 7. Forten refused to renounce his country.

_____ 8. Forten learned the trade of sail making.

WORKING WITH PRIMARY SOURCES

Read the words of Thomas Jefferson below. In your history journal, answer the questions that follow.

> [Lord Cornwallis] carried off about thirty slaves. Had this been to give them freedom, he would have done right; but it was to consign them to inevitable death from the smallpox and putrid fever then raging in his camp.

1. What is another way to say "consign them to inevitable death"?

2. What other groups do you think were suffering from "smallpox and putrid fever"?

3. Think about it: If Jefferson felt that Cornwallis's plan to free the slaves was "right," why didn't he free all of the slaves on his plantation? Write your thoughts in your history journal.

WRITING

Imagine you are a captured slave and that you can read and write. In your history journal, write a diary entry about your experience. Begin like this: "At first, I believed that the Redcoats offered us a chance to be free. But I soon learned otherwise." Continue with at least three more sentences.

SOLDIERS FROM EVERYWHERE

SUMMARY *The cause of liberty drew people from many nations and religions into the conflict. They contributed leadership, money, and, in some cases, their lives.*

BLACK SOLDIERS

SUMMARY *Virginians are forced to choose to rebel or to support the king when their royal governor proclaims "all indentured servants, Negroes, and others . . . free" if they are willing and able to defend the Crown.*

ACCESS

Chapter 24 introduces men from other countries that helped in the American Revolution. Chapter 25 discusses the role African Americans played in the Revolution. Copy the main idea map from page 8 of this guide into your history journal. In the large box, write "Soldiers from Everywhere." In the smaller boxes, write the names of the men who assisted in the American Revolution, the countries or colonies from which they came, and any other facts.

WORD BANK   drillmaster   dragoon   regulars   marquis (mar KEE)   recruits

Complete the sentences below with words from the word bank. One word is not used.

1. A _____ is a French nobleman.

2. A _____ works to make inexperienced _____ into trained _____.

3. A _____ might also be called a redcoat.

CRITICAL THINKING   DRAWING CONCLUSIONS

Each of the sentences in *italics* below is taken from the chapter. Put a check mark in front of the ONE conclusion that CANNOT be drawn from reading the lines.

1. *So when the American Revolution began, many of Europe's soldiers knocked on Ben Franklin's door.*

   _____ (a) Ben Franklin was a well-known American in Europe.

   _____ (b) Many European soldiers wanted to help the Americans fight the British.

   _____ (c) European soldiers also wanted to help the English fight against America.

2. *Von Steuben had a happy personality, a lot of energy, professional knowledge of soldiering, and a roaring voice.*

   _____ (a) Von Steuben was someone young soldiers would obey.

   _____ (b) Von Steuben was someone Washington could put into service.

   _____ (c) Von Steuben was someone who fought for personal wealth and glory.

3. *No one—black or white—knows where this rebellion will finally lead.*

   _____ (a) Not all colonists agreed with the men who wrote the Declaration of Independence.

   _____ (b) Blacks were more likely to side with the British.

   _____ (c) The first years of the Revolution were a time of uncertainty.

WORKING WITH PRIMARY SOURCES

Read Lafayette's words below. In your history journal, answer the questions that follow.

> As a defender of Liberty which I adore . . . coming to offer my services to this interesting republic, I am bringing nothing but my genuine goodwill.

1. How does Lafayette describe himself?

2. How does Lafayette describe America?

3. Would African Americans living in 1775 use the same words to describe America? Why or why not?

4. From reading the chapter, how do you know that Lafayette is being misleading when he says he is bringing "nothing but my goodwill"?

FIGHTING A WAR

SUMMARY *The opening battles of the war went badly for Washington. His strategy rested less on pursuing victory and more on avoiding capture.*

ACCESS

To organize this chapter's information, copy the outline graphic organizer from 8 of this study guide into your history journal. For the main idea, write *Fighting a War*. For details, write *Patriot difficulties*, *British military*, and *New York*. Put at least two points under each detail.

WORD BANK   desert   retreat   Hessians   mercenaries

Complete the sentences below with words from the word bank. One word is not used.

1. When faced with overwhelming force, the Patriot forces had to _____ to fight again.

2. German troops, called _____ were paid to fight for the British.

3. The use of paid soldiers or _____ enraged many colonists.

COMPREHENSION   MAIN IDEAS AND SUPPORTING DETAILS

Each sentence in *italics* below states a main idea from the chapter. Put a check mark in the blanks in front of the ONE sentence that DOES NOT support, or tell more about, the main idea.

1. *After Bunker Hill, Sullivan's Island, and Great Bridge nothing seemed to go right for the Americans.*

___ (a) Poor General Washington—no one else would have put up with all the hardships.

(b) Congress seemed to spend its time talking and not doing much else.

___ (c) In wintertime [the] soldiers almost froze—some actually did—and many didn't have shoes, or enough food to eat, or proper guns to use.

2. *For all his cool under fire, Washington was said to have had a fierce temper.*

___ (a) General Washington had his army in New York too.

___ (b) He must have had a hard time keeping it under control those first months after he took control.

___ (c) Everything seemed to go wrong.

3. *Most of the soldiers the Americans fought were not even British.*

___ (a) They were German—called Hessians—because many of them came from Hesse in Germany.

___ (b) Some German princes made money by supplying soldiers to anyone who wanted to pay for them.

___ (c) The British didn't just sit around and let the colonies rebel.

WORKING WITH PRIMARY SOURCES

Read the words of General Howe below. In your history journal, answer the questions that follow.

Their [the Americans'] want of judgment had shone equally conspicuous during the whole of this affair. They had imagined . . . that we should land directly in front of their works, march up and attack them without further precaution . . .

1. What does the word "want" mean in the statement above?

2. What does the word "works" mean in the statement above?

3. What does the word "precaution" mean in the statement above?

4. Rewrite the passage above in your own words.

WRITING

Imagine a new movie is about to be released in theaters, titled *Saratoga*. The film describes the events leading up to the colonial victory. Imagine you are an illustrator who's been asked to create the movie poster that will be used as an ad for the film. In your history journal, design a movie poster that shows the major characters.

HOWE BILLY WISHED FRANCE WOULDN'T JOIN IN

SUMMARY *The American victory at Saratoga changed the war. Sensing that the Americans could win, the French jumped in on their side.*

ACCESS

Copy the sequence of events chart from page 9 of this study guide into your history journal. The first event should be *Washington wins in Trenton and Princeton.* Fill in at least five more events from the information in the chapter.

WORD BANK   oath of allegiance   sniper   guerilla   sharpshooters

Complete the sentences below with words from the word bank. One word is not used.

1. After early defeats, some colonists took the _____ to obey the king.

2. After cutting trees to delay the British, Americans used _____ tactics to harass the troops.

3. A _____ in the bush could shoot the enemy redcoat without being seen.

WORD PLAY

Look up the word you didn't use in a dictionary. Find the sentence on page 129 that contains the word. Rewrite that sentence using the definition in place of the word itself.

MAP

Study the map from page 127. Answer the questions that follow.

1. Burgoyne split up his forces after leaving _____.

   ___(a) Fort Stanwix _____ (b) Fort Ticonderoga __ (c) Fort Edward

2. The British force from the west turned back after the battle at _____.

   ___ (a) New York _____ (b) Bennington _____ (c) Fort Stanwix

3. Instead of moving _____ up the Hudson River, Howe marched _____ toward Philadelphia.

   _____ (a) north, south _____ (b) south, east _____ (a) north, east

4. Before Saratoga, British forces were defeated at _____ and _____.

   ____ (a) New York, Fort Ticonderoga _____ (b) Fort Stanwix, Bennington ____ (c) Albany, Fort Edward

CRITICAL THINKING   CAUSE AND EFFECT

Draw a line between the cause on the left and its effect on the right. There is one extra effect.

1. Washington crossed the Delaware River.

2. Howe led his army to Philadelphia.

3. Burgoyne decided to fight the Americans.

4. Burgoyne and his army surrendered at Saratoga.

a. The French decided to join the American cause.

b. The Hessians were defeated at Trenton and Princeton.

c. Howe spent the winter in New York.

d. Burgoyne's plan to trap the Americans changed.

e. American sharpshooters destroyed Burgoyne's force.

WRITING

Imagine that you are the American official who must write to Ben Franklin about the Patriot victory. In your history journal, write the letter that brings the good news. Begin like this: "To the Honorable Mr. Franklin—There is great news from here in America."

VALLEY FORGE TO VINCENNES

SUMMARY *The hardships of the war gave Washington a battle-tested army. After Valley Forge, these troops began a campaign to sweep the British and their mercenaries off the continent.*

ACCESS

This chapter discusses two important locations of the Revolution. In your history journal, make a timeline of the years 1777 and 1778. Divide the years into months. Begin with the Battle of Saratoga from chapter 27. Continue with the battles that Washington lost during the winter of 1777 to 1778, and conclude with the battle of Vincennes. Write as much information as you can about each event.

MAP

Use the map of the Revolutionary War battles in the Atlas section of your book. Find the two locations discussed in the chapter, Valley Forge and Vincennes.

1. How many miles apart are they from each other? _____

2. Which rivers or other bodies of water could have been used to transport soldiers? _____

WORD BANK   mutiny   quartermaster   serfs   surveyor

Complete the sentences below with words from the word bank. One word is not used.

1. A _____ obtains food and clothing for troops.

2. Without proper food and clothing, troops may rebel or _____.

3. Poor farmers, known as _____, struggled to survive in Poland.

WORD PLAY

Look up the remaining word in a dictionary. Then, find a sentence in chapter 28 that contains that word. Rewrite that sentence using the definition in place of the word itself.

WORKING WITH PRIMARY SOURCES

Read the diary entry of Dr. Albigence Waldo below. In your history journal, answer the questions that follow.

Dec. 14th Poor food—hard lodging—cold weather—fatigue—nasty clothes—nasty cookery—vomit half my time—smoked out of my senses . . . why are we sent here to starve and freeze[?]

1. What do you think Waldo means by the term "hard lodging"?

2. What do you think is the difference between "nasty clothes" and "nasty cookery"?

3. Why do you think Waldo felt "smoked out of [his] senses"?

4. How would you answer Waldo's final question?

WRITING

Imagine that you are a soldier at Valley Forge. You are as miserable as Waldo, but one cold night Washington joins your campfire for a few moments. Write a diary entry in your history journal about the encounter. Illustrate it with drawings or with a parent or partner or group, make a storyboard with words and pictures.

THE STATES WRITE CONSTITUTIONS

SUMMARY *The principles that shaped the Constitution of the United States found their first expression in written documents produced at the state level. Two overarching concerns guided the authors' pens: protection from the abuses of power and guarantees of liberty.*

ACCESS

To help yourself understand the importance of states' constitutions, make a K-W-L graphic organizer in your history journal like the one on page 8 of this study guide. In the "What I *Know*" column, write what you know about constitutions. Then, skim through the chapter, looking at illustrations and maps, and think of what you'd like to find out. In the "What I *Want* to Know" column, write five questions you have about the purpose of a constitution. After you read the chapter, fill out the "What I *Learned*" column with answers to your questions and other information about constitutions.

WORD BANK

| separation of powers | legislative branch | judicial branch |
| executive branch | constitution | |

Complete the sentences below with words from the word bank. One word is not used.

1. The _____ was also called an assembly.

2. The _____ divides the job of governing into three parts.

3. The _____ was made up of the courts.

4. The _____ was also called the governor.

MAKING INFERENCES

Each sentence below expresses a concern that colonists had about their government. Put a check in front of the right or freedom that is described.

1. All children should be allowed to go to a school that is funded by the state.

_____ (a) freedom of the press _____ (b) free education _____ (c) voting rights

2. Newspapers should be allowed to criticize the governor or the assembly.

_____ (a) voting rights _____ (b) majority rule _____ (c) freedom of the press

3. All men should be allowed to decide who represents them in the assembly.

_____ (a) freedom of speech _____ (b) voting rights _____ (c) freedom of religion

4. No one has the right to force a person to worship in a certain way.

_____ (a) freedom of religion _____ (b) free education _____ (c) majority rule

5. No one can be prevented from expressing his or her opinion, no matter how offensive it may be.

_____ (a) majority rule _____ (b) freedom of religion _____ (c) freedom of speech

WORKING WITH PRIMARY SOURCES

Read the words of James Madison below. In your history journal, answer the questions that follow.

> It is the first instance, from the creation of the world . . . that free inhabitants have been seen deliberating on a form of government.

1. What do the words "from the creation of the world" mean?

2. Who are the "inhabitants" that Madison is writing about?

3. What is another word for "deliberating"?

4. What "form of government" do you think Madison is writing about?

WRITING

Imagine you were making a "class constitution." What are the most important rights that all students should have? In your history journal, make a bill of five rules that you believe would help "govern" your class. (Share ideas with classmates.)

MORE ABOUT CHOICES

SUMMARY *In the western part of the continent, Spanish settlers were leaving their mark on the lands destined to become part of the United States. In the East, individuals such as Mary Katherine Goddard set precedents that would one day be shared by all people who called themselves American.*

ACCESS

In your history journal, use an outline graphic organizer like the one on page 8 of this study guide to organize the information in this chapter. The three main ideas are *New Spain*, *Henry Knox*, and *Mary Katherine Goddard*. Write at least two details under each main idea.

WORD BANK   press   satire   irony

Use one of the words above twice in the sentences below. Don't use one at all.

_____ is a form of humor that often uses _____. _____ means saying one thing when you mean the opposite.

Write a sentence using the leftover word that also uses these words: *printing, important, Revolution, message.*

_____

_____

CRITICAL THINKING   FACT OR OPINION

A fact is a statement that can be proven. An opinion is a belief that may or may not be true. Label each sentence below F or O.

_____ 1. Decisions . . . decisions . . . they aren't easy.

_____ 2. Henry Knox was 12 when his father died; it was up to Henry to support his mother.

_____ 3. A militia is a volunteer force of citizen-soldiers.

_____ 4. Henry Knox was a happy-natured fellow who rarely got discouraged.

_____ 5. Knox and his artillery served in almost every major battle of the Revolution.

_____ 6. Mary Katherine Goddard would never have swallowed a chicken bone.

_____ 7. Mary Katherine became an expert printer.

_____ 8. Mary Katherine Goddard became postmistress of Baltimore—until her job was given to a man.

WORKING WITH PRIMARY SOURCES

Read the words of Lucy Flucker Knox below. In your history journal, answer the questions that follow.

> I hope you will not consider yourself as commander-in-chief in your own house, but be convinced . . . that there is such a thing as equal command.

1. What is another way to say "commander-in-chief"?

2. How would a person who was considered "commander in chief" in his or her "own house" act to other family members?

3. What do you think Lucy Knox means by "equal command"?

WRITING

Imagine that you are Lucy Knox (or you agree with her about "equal command") and you learn that Mary Katherine Goddard has lost her job as postmistress to a man. In your history journal, write a letter to the mayor of Baltimore expressing your feelings about the situation.

WHEN IT'S OVER, SHOUT HOORAY

SUMMARY *With the help of France, the Americans finally backed the British into a corner at Yorktown. The fife and drum played a tune that summed up American victory: "The World Turned Upside Down."*

ACCESS

In your history journal, make a timeline like the one on page 9 of this guide. Make each event a battle that you have read about in the preceding chapters. Begin with the battles at Lexington and Concord. When you finish this chapter, enter the final major battle of the war: Yorktown.

WORD BANK   stalemated

In a dictionary, look up the word above. Then find the sentence on page 142 that contains the word. Rewrite that sentence using the definition in place of the word itself.

CRITICAL THINKING   SEQUENCE OF EVENTS

Write a "B" in the blank if the event described took place *before* the surrender at Yorktown. Write an "A" if the event took place *after* the surrender at Yorktown.

_____ 1. Delegates from England and the United States sign the Treaty of Paris.

_____ 2. Cornwallis won battles at Charleston and Camden in South Carolina.

_____ 3. De Grasse blockaded the Chesapeake Bay with French warships.

_____ 4. About 100,000 Loyalists moved to Canada.

_____ 5. An American-French army marched south from Rhode Island.

_____ 6. British soldiers marched between a line of French and American troops to lay down their arms.

_____ 7. The *Bonhomme Richard* warship commanded by John Paul Jones defeated the British warship *Serapis*.

_____ 8. England returned Florida to Spain.

WORKING WITH PRIMARY SOURCES

Read the words of Benjamin Rush below. In your history journal, answer the questions that follow.

> The American war is over, but this is far from being the case with the American Revolution. Nothing but the first act of the drama is closed.

1. After what battle do you think Rush wrote these words?

2. What do you think Rush means by the term "American Revolution"?

3. To Rush, what is the difference between a war and a revolution?

4. What is the "drama" that Rush is writing about?

WRITING

Make a "to do" list of five important tasks for the new nation that has just gained freedom from England. Keep the list in your history journal. As you read about the leaders of our young country accomplishing the tasks you have set out, make a check mark and note the year it was accomplished.

EXPERIMENTING WITH A NATION

SUMMARY *When the Revolution ended, few Americans talked of the United States. Unity took the form of the loose association of states created by the Articles of Confederation. Its weakness paved the way for a new government—a federal republic.*

ACCESS

To organize the information in this chapter, copy a main idea map from page 8 of this study guide into your history journal. Write *Articles of Confederation* in the large circle. As you read about the problems that arose in unifying the colonies, write about them in the smaller circles.

WORD BANK

supply and demand   inflation   Articles of Confederation   parliament

Complete the sentences below with words from the word bank. One word is not used.

1. Under the _____, each colony printed its own money.

2. Under the law of _____, too much money meant that its value went down.

3. Too much money in use led to the economic problem of _____ .

CRITICAL THINKING   DRAWING CONCLUSIONS

Each of the sentences in *italics* below is taken from the chapter. Put a check mark in front of the ONE conclusion that CANNOT be drawn from reading the lines.

1. *Each state was printing its own money and making its own rules.*

_____ (a) Some states were wealthier than other states.

_____ (b) Some states had stricter laws than others.

_____ (c) Some states tried to rule other states.

2. *The national government, under the Articles of Confederation, was just too weak.*

_____ (a) A national government is made up of all of the states.

_____ (b) Americans wanted to return to English rule.

_____ (c) Americans were worried about giving too much power to a national government.

3. *But most people still thought of themselves first as citizens of the state they lived in.*

_____ (a) Americans were not patriotic.

_____ (b) People from different regions had little in common.

_____ (c) As citizens, they were allowed to vote in their state's political elections.

MAP

Study the map on page 148 of your book. In your history journal, answer the questions that follow.

1. Which state claimed the most territory west of the Ohio River?

2. Which states did not claim any territory?

3. Which state claimed the territory that was farthest west?

4. Which states claimed territory that they bordered on directly?

WRITING

Imagine that you are a newspaper editor in a state that does not claim any western territory. In your history journal, write an editorial in which you criticize your state's government for failing to expand.

LOOKING NORTHWEST

SUMMARY *The one triumph of the national government under the Articles of Confederation was the passage of the Northwest Ordinance. This law helped ensure the orderly expansion of the United States through the admission of states on an equal footing with the rest of the nation.*

ACCESS

This chapter describes the beginning of westward movement in the 1780s. In your history journal, make a cause and effect chart like the one on page 9 of this study guide. For the first cause, write "Virginia and Georgia cede northwest land claims." Follow up with at least four links in a cause-and-effect chain.

WORD BANK   ordinance   Northwest Ordinance   townships   Conestoga   involuntary servitude

Complete the sentences below with words from the word bank. One word is not used.

1. _____, or being forced to work, was outlawed by the _____, an act passed by Congress.

2. The law, or _____, passed by Congress also established rules for making areas called

_____ into states.

3. After the passage of the new laws, thousands of settlers moved west in covered wagons that were called

_____ wagons after the place they were made.

COMPREHENSION   MAIN IDEA AND SUPPORTING DETAILS

Each sentence in *italics* below states a main idea from the chapter. Put a check mark in the blanks in front of the ONE sentence that DOES NOT support or tell more about each main idea sentence.

1. *Virginia gave up enough land in the Northwest Territory to make the future states of Ohio, Illinois, Indiana, Michigan, Wisconsin, and part of Minnesota.*

_____ (a) That congress did a few things right, and the Northwest Ordinance was one of them.

_____ (b) Without Virginia to claim it, that land was like a colony belonging to thirteen states.

_____ (c) Now colonies throughout history had existed for the benefit of the mother country.

2. *A system was devised for dividing the land into areas called townships.*

_____ (a) Groups of townships could become states.

_____ (b) Great Britain had tried to keep settlers out of the western territories.

_____ (c) That system worked so well it was used again and again as the nation grew.

3. *No one knew how many settlers were moving over the Appalachians—the first census did not come until 1790—but thousands and thousands were on their way west.*

_____ (a) Many piled their families and belongings into big wooden-wheeled wagons and hitched them to oxen.

_____ (b) The ordinance provided another important guarantee.

_____ (c) They were called covered wagons because they had canvas tops that were stretched over wooden rods.

WRITING

Imagine you were alive in the 1780s. Make a list of five rights that you would have insisted on for all people moving west. Record your list in your history journal.

CHAPTER 34 A MAN WITH IDEAS

SUMMARY *Thomas Jefferson designed houses, inventions, and principles of government. The idea of the separation of church and state owes its origins to Thomas Jefferson and his friend James Madison.*

ACCESS

To organize information from this chapter, draw a K-W-L graphic organizer in your history journal like the one on page 8 of this study guide. In the "What I Know" column, write what you know about Thomas Jefferson. Then, skim through the chapter, looking at illustrations and maps, and think of what you'd like to find out. In the "What I Want to Know" column, write five questions you have about Jefferson. After you read the chapter, fill in the "What I Learned" column with answers to your questions and other information about this famous American.

WORD BANK   intellectual   piedmont   decimal system   statute   separation of church and state

Complete the sentences below with words from the word bank. One word is not used.

1. Monticello was located in the _____ or foothills of Virginia.

2. The _____ was an important step in religious freedom.

3. Jefferson's support of a money system based on the _____ was one of many contributions of this well-educated _____.

CRITICAL THINKING   MAKING INFERENCES

Put an "A" in front of the sentences below that describe Jefferson's ideas about architecture. Put an "F" in front of his ideas about farming. Put a "G" in front of his ideas about government. Put an "R" in front of his ideas about human rights.

_____ 1. He tried to get Virginia to adopt his plan for general education.

_____ 2. Inside are doors that seem to swing by magic—Jefferson designed them.

_____ 3. He stocked the pond with fish and the gardens with unusual flowers, fruits, vines, and trees.

_____ 4. He tried to end slavery in Virginia.

_____ 5. In other words, a government and its citizens' religions should be separated.

_____ 6. But as a slave owner, he never freed his slaves.

_____ 7. He meant for people to be free to believe whatever they wished.

_____ 8. It was Jefferson who insisted on a money system for the United States based on tens.

WORKING WITH PRIMARY SOURCES

Read the words of George Washington below. In your history journal, answer the questions that follow.

> In this Land of equal liberty it is our boast, that a man's religious tenets will not . . . deprive him of the right of . . . holding the highest Offices that are known in the United States.

1. What does Washington mean by the term "this Land"?

2. What is another way to say "it is our boast"?

3. What is another way to say "a man's religious tenets"?

IN YOUR OWN WORDS

Rewrite Washington's opinion in more modern language in your history journal.

A PHILADELPHIA WELCOME

SUMMARY *Led by James Madison, the Virginians traveled to the Constitutional Convention armed with ideas for change. Instead of revising the Articles of Confederation, delegates found themselves debating a new proposal, the so-called Virginia Plan.*

SIGNING UP

SUMMARY *In public, delegates eagerly enjoyed the charms of Philadelphia. Meanwhile, ordinary Philadelphians knew nothing of the bitter conflicts taking place each day behind the locked doors of the Pennsylvania State House.*

ACCESS

In your history journal, use a main idea map, like the one on page 8 of this study guide, to organize the information in this chapter. Put *Philadelphia 1787* in the large circle. Make four smaller circles and label them *Who?, What?, When?,* and *Why?* Enter the information from the two chapters that answer those questions.

WORD BANK
Constitutional Convention   Virginia Plan   median   Framers   debates

Complete the sentences below with words from the word bank. One word is not used.

1. James Madison helped to write the _____.

2. Madison brought his work to the _____.

3. At age thirty-six, he was above the _____ age of all colonists, half of whom were younger than sixteen.

4. One of the _____ of the Constitution, Madison was largely responsible for creating the document that outlines the U.S. government.

CRITICAL THINKING   FACT OR OPINION

A fact is a statement that can be proven. An opinion is a belief that may or may not be true. Label each sentence below F or O.

_____ 1. Everyone agreed that Philadelphia was the most modern city in America, perhaps in the world.

_____ 2. Philadelphia, with 40,000 people, was the largest city in America.

_____ 3. James Madison was one of the first delegates to arrive in Philadelphia, but no one paid him attention.

_____ 4. Jemmy Madison was the oldest of twelve children born to a plantation-owning Virginia Piedmont family.

_____ 5. Jefferson sent Madison books—hundreds of books—and he sent his ideas.

_____ 6. The fifty-five delegates all made it through the Philadelphia summer, so they must have been strong men.

_____ 7. It was a good thing that James Madison was so well-prepared.

_____ 8. James Madison has been called the Father of the Constitution.

WORKING WITH PRIMARY SOURCES

Read William Pierce's description of James Madison below. In your history journal, answer the questions that follow. Feel free to circle important or unfamiliar words as you read.

> Mr. Madison . . . blends . . . the profound politician with the scholar . . . and though he cannot be called an orator, he is a most agreeable, eloquent, and convincing speaker.

1. What words above tell you that Pierce admired Madison?

2. What kind of speaker is one who is "agreeable"?

3. Why would an "eloquent" speaker make listeners think he or she was a "scholar"?

4. Why would a "convincing" speaker be a good politician?

CHAPTER 37

A SLAP ON THE BACK

SUMMARY *Many issues divided the delegates, but the most explosive one was of power. Some delegates wanted strong state governments; others wanted a strong national government. Out of the debate came a compromise: a federal system of shared power.*

ACCESS

In your history journal, use an outline graphic organizer, like the one on page 8 of this study guide, to organize the information in this chapter. The three main ideas are *Delegates*, *Federations*, and *Confederation*. Write at least two facts under each main idea.

WORD BANK   confederation   federation   federal   federalism   sumptuous

Complete the sentences below with words from the word bank. One word is not used.

1. A _____ is a form of government that divides power between a central government and state governments.

2. The _____ government is the central government for a country.

3. A _____ is a government made up of partners.

4. Those who supported _____ were opposed to a government of partners.

CRITICAL THINKING   MAKING INFERENCES

Write an F in front of the sentences below that refer to a federal government. Write a C in front of the sentences that refer to a confederation.

_____ 1. Hamilton wanted a strong central government.

_____ 2. Hamilton wanted the president to have a lifetime job—like a king or emperor.

_____ 3. John Dickinson, or Delaware, was for strong states.

_____ 4. The central government served mainly as an adviser.

_____ 5. The central government in Washington has the strongest powers, but not all the power.

WORKING WITH PRIMARY SOURCES

Read the words of John Dickinson below. In your history journal, answer the questions that follow.

> Let the general government be like the sun and the states like the planets, repelled yet attracted, and the whole moving regularly and harmoniously in several orbits.

1. In Dickinson's view, which part of the solar system is like the federal government?

2. In Dickinson's view, which part of the solar system is like a confederation?

3. In what ways, do you think, are people who favor confederation "repelled" by the sun?

4. In what ways, do you think, are people who favor federalism "attracted" by the sun?

WRITING

In your history journal, write a letter to John Dickinson in which you respond to his "solar system" comparison. Begin like this: "Mr. Dickinson, I am impressed by your 'solar system' ideal of government. In my opinion, I'd rather be governed by . . . [choose either the sun or a planet]."

ROGER TO THE RESCUE

SUMMARY *Another conflict over power erupted when big and little states battled over representation. Roger Sherman settled the matter with a compromise that created the bicameral legislature.*

JUST WHAT IS A CONSTITUTION?

SUMMARY *The Framers intended the Constitution to be the supreme law of the land. Their gift to future generations was a provision for amendment so that the document could change with the times.*

ACCESS

To organize information from this chapter, make a K-W-L graphic organizer in your history journal. See page 8 of this study guide for an example. Then, skim through the chapter, looking at illustrations and maps, and think of what you'd like to find out. In the "What I *Know*" column, write what you know about the Constitution. (Review Chapters 35 and 37 to remind yourself). Then, skim through the chapter, looking at illustrations and maps, and think of what you'd like to find out. In the "What I *Want* to Know" column, write five questions you have about the Constitution. After you read the chapter, fill out the "What I *Learned*" column with answers to your questions and other information about the Constitution.

WORD BANK

Three-Fifths Compromise	Virginia Plan	New Jersey Plan
Connecticut Plan	Great Compromise	checks and balances
supreme law	amendments	ratify

Complete the sentences below with words from the word bank.

1. The _____, which was based on population, was the opposite of the

   _____, which gave each state an equal number of representatives.

2. The _____ of Roger Sherman also became known as the _____.

3. The _____ addressed the issue of counting the slave population in Southern states.

4. With its system of _____ for all three branches of government, the U.S. Constitution became the

   _____ of the nation.

5. One of the key ingredients in creating the constitution was creating a place for _____ or changes to the document.

6. Once the delegates had approved the Constitution, it was sent to the states for them to _____.

WORKING WITH PRIMARY SOURCES

Read the words of Roger Sherman below. In your history journal, answer the questions that follow.

> The people should have as little to do as may be about the Government. They want information and are constantly liable to be misled.

1. What is another way to say "as little to do as may be"?

2. One meaning of the word "want" is "lack." How does that make sense in Sherman's second sentence?

3. Did Sherman trust the average American to make wise decisions about government? Why or why not?

WRITING

In your history journal, write a letter to Roger Sherman expressing your disagreement with his opinion. Begin like this: "To the Honorable R. Sherman. Sir, I believe that you think too little of the average American. We wish to participate in your government."

CHAPTER 40

GOOD WORDS AND BAD

SUMMARY *The Constitution contains flaws, especially the provisions dealing with slavery. But the words "We the People" held out an ideal for perfection. Through the amendment process, Americans have reached for that ideal.*

ACCESS

In your history journal, make a cause-and-effect chart like the one on page 9 to organize the information about slavery and the Constitution. Begin with the words from the Declaration of Independence: . . . *all men are created equal* . . . What effect did those words have on the delegates to the Constitutional Convention who opposed slavery? How did the views of those in opposition to slavery influence the men who held slaves? Try to make a cause-and-effect chain with at least six links.

WORD BANK

Preamble   slave trade   cotton gin   paradox

Complete the sentences below with words from the word bank. One word is not used.

1. The first words of the Constitution are called the _____.

2. The _____ brought Africans to America.

3. The _____ made keeping Africans in slavery profitable for many Southerners.

MAIN IDEA AND SUPPORTING DETAILS

Each sentence in *italics* below states a main idea from the chapter. Put a check mark in the blanks in front of the ONE statement that DOES NOT support or tell more about the main idea.

1. *Those Founders—most of them, anyway—were idealistic men.*

_____ (a) They were thinkers who were ahead of their times.

_____ (b) They knew they were writing for future generations.

_____ (c) The Constitution was different from the Declaration of Independence.

2. *They had to create a working document that people would approve.*

_____ (a) And they knew that some of the people weren't prepared to do things that had never been done before.

_____ (b) But when the Framers said "we the people," did they really mean all the people?

_____ (c) So, many of the delegates acted as if "we the people" meant "we the grown-up white men who own property."

3. *Most of the delegates didn't want slavery.*

_____ (a) But in the South—especially in South Carolina and Georgia—a way of life depended on slave labor.

_____ (b) The slave trade was the business of bringing Africans into the country and selling them as slaves.

_____ (c) The citizens of those states would not approve the Constitution if it prohibited slavery.

WORKING WITH PRIMARY SOURCES

Read the opening words, the Preamble, to the Constitution. In your history journal, answer the questions that follow.

> We the People of the United States, in order to form a more perfect union, establish justice, ensure domestic tranquility, provide for the common defence, promote the general welfare, and secure the blessings of liberty to ourselves and our posterity, do ordain and establish this Constitution for the United States of America.

To help understand the wording in the Preamble, divide it into small bits. Draw a circle each phrase set off by a comma. There should be eight total. Then, in your history journal, make a two column chart. In the left column, list the eight phrases. In the right column, brainstorm and take notes on what you think each phrase means. Then, rewrite the Preamble in your own words, using the notes you wrote.

NO MORE SECRETS

SUMMARY *Each delegate had reservations about the Constitution, but few believed any better plan could be devised. They turned the plan over to the states for ratification, triggering yet another round of conflict and debate.*

ACCESS

This chapter discusses the secret meetings of the constitutional delegates over the summer of 1787. To organize the information, go back to the main idea map that you created for chapters 35 and 36 in your history journal. In that graphic organizer, you wrote *Philadelphia 1787* in the large circle and made four smaller circles and label them *Who?*, *What?*, *When?*, and *Why?* As you read this chapter, enter any additional information that adds to what you learned from those chapters.

WORD BANK   ratification

In a dictionary, look up the meaning of the word above. Find the sentence in chapter 41 that uses the word in the form of a verb. Rewrite that sentence using the meaning rather than the word itself.

MAKING INFERENCES

Write an "R" in front of the sentences below if you think the speaker favors ratification of the Constitution. Write a "D" if you think the speaker wants to defeat the Constitution.

_____ 1. "It should be we the states, not we the people!"

_____ 2. "I will not compromise with my desire to abolish the slave trade."

_____ 3. "The sun is rising over this effort to form a united government."

_____ 4. "I smell a rat in Philadelphia."

_____ 5. "Half a loaf is better than no bread at all."

_____ 6. "I would rather go hungry than accept these crumbs."

_____ 7. "Your liberties will be safe."

_____ 8. "This system approaches perfection."

WORKING WITH PRIMARY SOURCES

Read the words from the Maryland Journal below. In your history journal, answer the questions that follow. Go back to the book as much as you want.

> The members of the . . . convention should have seized the happy opportunity of prohibiting forever this cruel species of reprobated villainy.

1. What is another word for "members"?

2. What "happy opportunity" is the writer referring to?

3. What is a modern way to say "this cruel species of reprobated villainy"?

4. Looking back at the chapter, how would George Mason feel about this statement?

WRITING

In your history journal, write a letter to the editor of the *Maryland Journal* in which you either agree or disagree with his opinion. If you agree, say whether you think the Constitution still deserves to be ratified. If you disagree, explain that abolishing slavery would have itself "prohibited" the ratification of the constitution.

CHAPTER 42

IF YOU CAN KEEP IT

SUMMARY *As soon as Americans saw the newly written Constitution, they set out to improve it. The price of ratification was a promise to add the ten amendments known today as the Bill of Rights.*

ACCESS

In your history journal, make a timeline graphic organizer of the ten-year period from 1781 to 1791. (See page 9 of this study guide or page 202 of your book for an example.) Review chapters 31 to 41 to find important dates for the timeline. Add the information to the earlier timelines you have prepared for the period before and during the American Revolution. When you have finished, look up the dates of George Washington's birth and death. Write his age next to the important dates. Do the same for Franklin, Adams, Jefferson, Madison, and Hamilton.

WORD BANK   Bill of Rights   republic   Anti-Federalist   militia

Complete the sentences below with words from the word bank. One word is not used.

1. A _____ is a government whose leaders are elected by the people.

2. The _____ was added to the Constitution to satisfy concerns of some state legislatures.

3. An _____ would not support a strong federal government.

CRITICAL THINKING   FACT OR OPINION

A fact is a statement that can be proven. An opinion is a belief that may or may not be true. Label each sentence below F or O.

_____ 1. Jefferson wrote from Paris to Madison and Washington that a bill of rights was needed.

_____ 2. Most people agree: the First Amendment is the most important part of the Bill of Rights.

_____ 3. The Third Amendment says soldiers can't be quartered in your house without your consent.

_____ 4. Henry and Hamilton were gracious in their actions, and that became the American way.

_____ 5. In this country, when a candidate loses an election for president, he doesn't become spiteful or nasty.

_____ 6. People can't be trusted to govern themselves.

_____ 7. Jefferson knew that self-rule depends on informed citizens.

WORKING WITH PRIMARY SOURCES

Read the closing words of the Declaration of Independence. In your history journal, answer the questions that follow.

> . . .with a firm Reliance on the Protection of divine Providence, we mutually pledge to each other our Lives, our Fortunes, and our sacred Honor.

1. What religious term does the declaration use for a higher power?

2. Why did the men who signed the declaration know that they were pledging their "Lives"?

3. Why did they understand they were risking their "Fortunes"?

4. What do you think they meant by "sacred Honor"?

WRITING

Think back on the stories you read in this book. Which one stands out as being memorable? In your history journal, retell the most memorable story from the book with pictures or in words.

NAME _____

LIBRARY / MEDIA CENTER RESEARCH LOG   **DUE DATE** _____

What I Need to **Find**

I need to use:

☐ primary
☐ secondary   sources.

☐ Book/Periodical
☐ Website
☐ Other

☐☐☐☐☐☐ (checkbox columns)

Places I **Know** to Look

WHAT I FOUND

Title/Author/Location (call # or URL)

☐ Primary Source
☐ Secondary Source

Brainstorm: Other Sources and Places to Look

How I Found it

☐ Suggestion
☐ Library Catalog
☐ Browsing
☐ Internet Search
☐ Web link

Rate each source from 1 (low) to 4 (high) in the categories below

helpful

relevant

LIBRARY / MEDIA CENTER RESEARCH LOG

NAME _____   DUE DATE _____

What I Need to Find

I need to use:
- ☐ primary
- ☐ secondary

sources.

Places I **Know** to Look

Brainstorm: Other Sources and Places to Look

WHAT I FOUND

Title/Author/Location (call # or URL)

	How I Found it							Rate each source from 1 (low) to 4 (high) in the categories below
Book/Periodical	Website	Other	Suggestion	Library Catalog	Browsing	Internet Search	Web link	Primary Source	Secondary Source	helpful	relevant

NAME _____

LIBRARY / MEDIA CENTER RESEARCH LOG

DUE DATE _____

What I Need to **Find**

Places I **Know** to Look

Brainstorm: Other Sources and Places to Look

I need to use:

☐ primary
☐ secondary

sources.

WHAT I FOUND

Title/Author/Location (call # or URL)

☐ Book/Periodical
☐ Website
☐ Other

☐ Primary Source
☐ Secondary Source

How I Found it

☐ Suggestion
☐ Library Catalog
☐ Browsing
☐ Internet Search
☐ Web link

Rate each source from 1 (low) to 4 (high) in the categories below

helpful

relevant

LIBRARY/ MEDIA CENTER RESEARCH LOG

NAME _____

DUE DATE _____

What I Need to Find

I need to use: [ ]
- [ ] primary sources.
- [ ] secondary

Places I **Know** to Look

Brainstorm: Other Sources and Places to Look

WHAT I FOUND

Title/Author/Location (call # or URL)

How I Found it

- Suggestion
- Library Catalog
- Browsing
- Internet Search
- Web link

- Primary Source
- Secondary Source

- Book/Periodical
- Website
- Other

Rate each source from 1 (low) to 4 (high) in the categories below

helpful   relevant

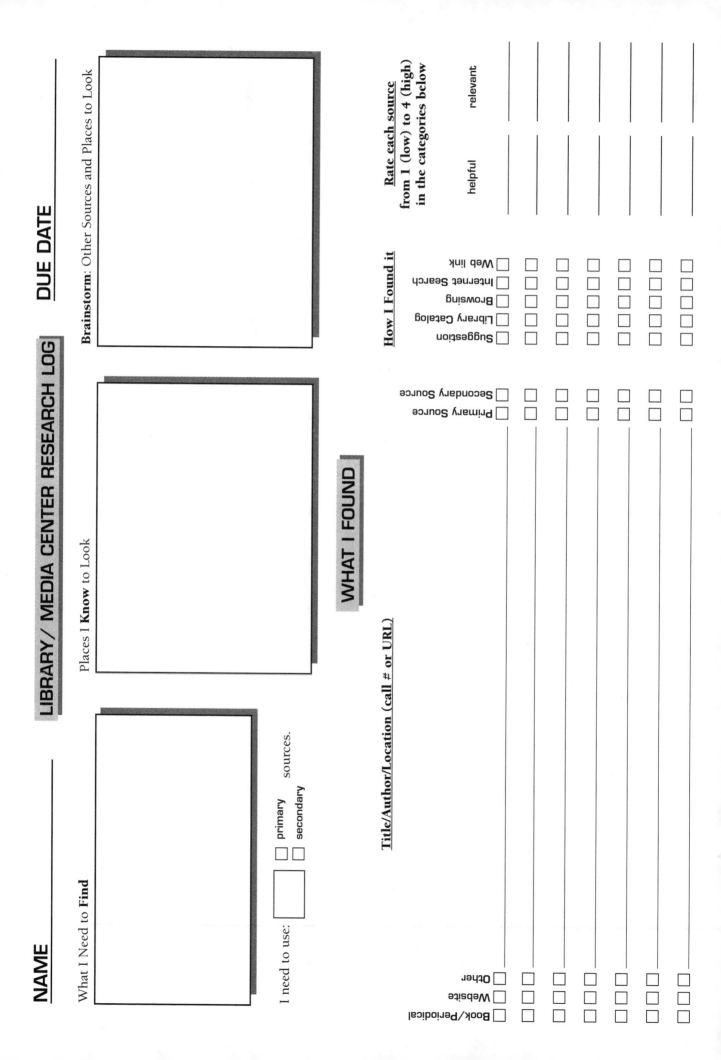

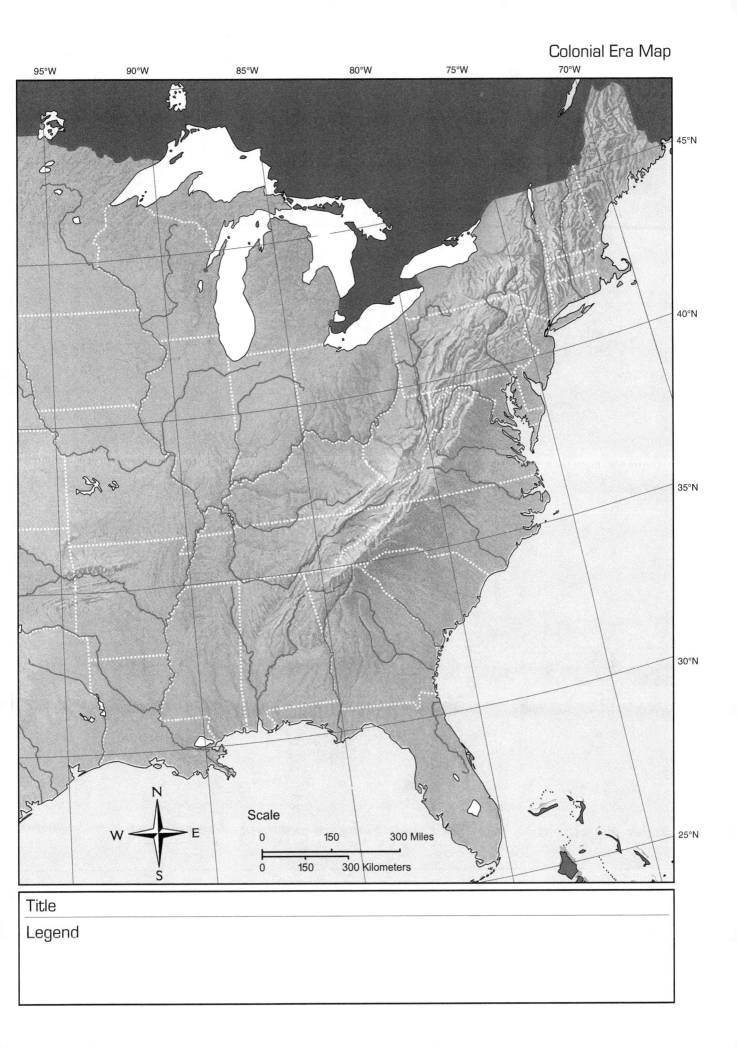

Colonial Era Map

Scale

0   150   300 Miles

0   150   300 Kilometers

Title

Legend

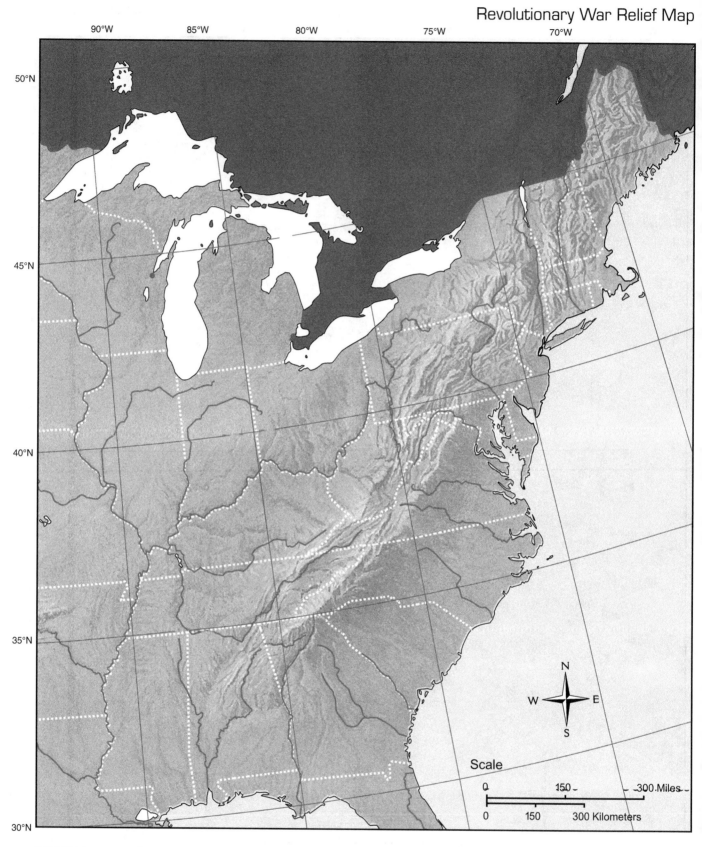

90°W   85°W   80°W   75°W   70°W

50°N

45°N

40°N

35°N

30°N

Scale

N
W — E
S

0   150   300 Miles
0   150   300 Kilometers

Title

Legend

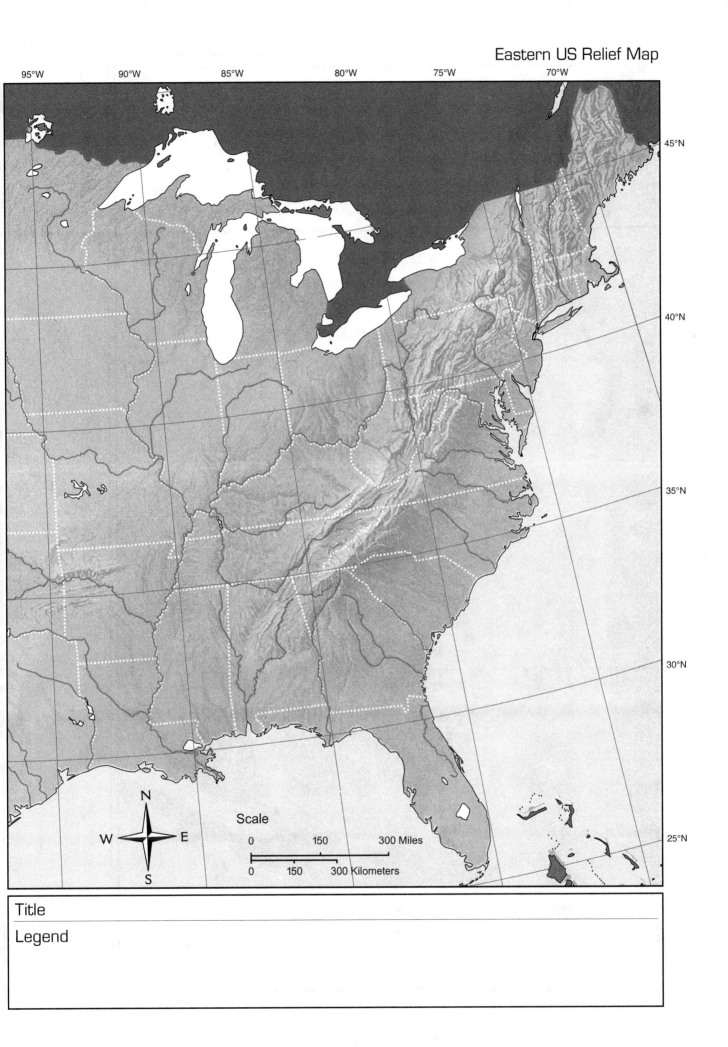

Eastern US Relief Map

95°W 90°W 85°W 80°W 75°W 70°W

45°N

40°N

35°N

30°N

25°N

Scale

N
W ✦ E
S

0   150   300 Miles

0   150   300 Kilometers

Title

Legend

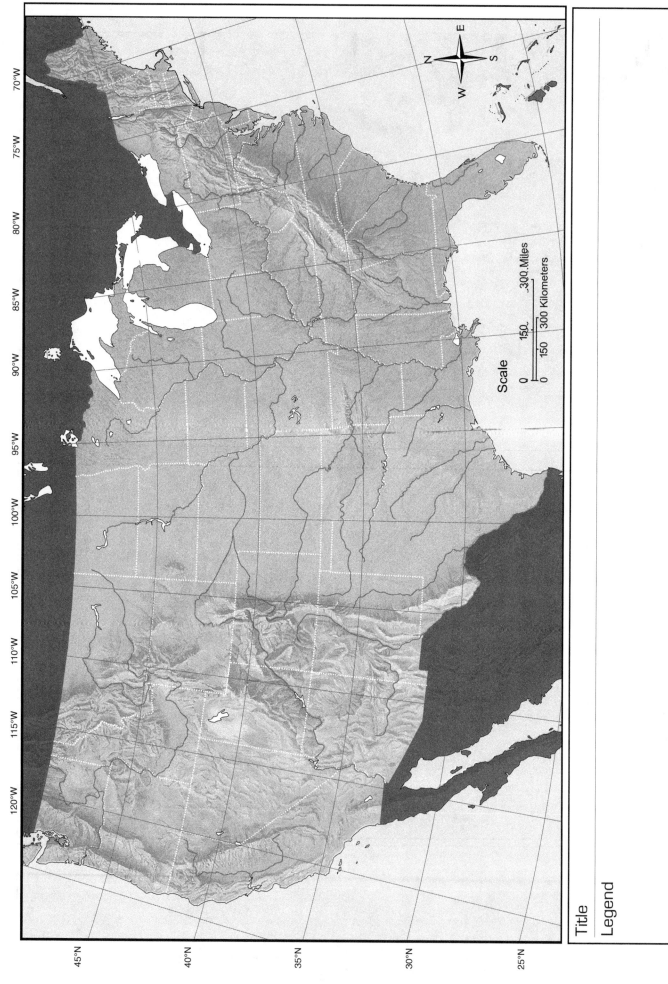

70°W
75°W
80°W
85°W
90°W
95°W
100°W
105°W
110°W
115°W
120°W

45°N
40°N
35°N
30°N
25°N

N
E
S
W

Scale

0   150   300 Miles
0   150   300 Kilometers

Title

Legend

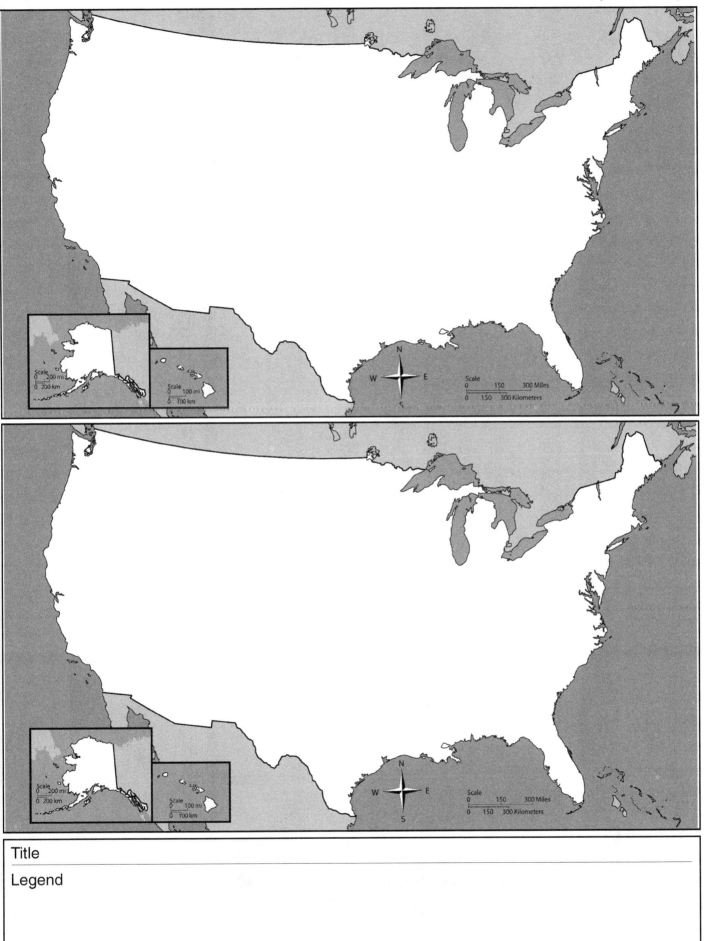

Title

Legend

Title

Legend

Printed in the USA
CPSIA information can be obtained
at www.ICGtesting.com
CBHW061235040124
2927CB00008B/6